MY MARRIED
MODERN
MONASTIC LIFE

Cover Photo: Franciscan Monk, Verna Monastery, Public Domain

Bonsai Tree: istock photo 154889951 with standard license

Just Breathe: istock photo 649430140 with standard license

All other photos: From the many years of work of Agape Unlimited in Russia with many taken by me on my many trips to Russia

ISPN:

    Kindle: 978-1-7338912-0-2
    Print: 978-1-7338912-1-9

Cross-Staff Ministries

Acknowledgements

For my loving wife Cindy, who has shared with me the comfort of unwavering love and my good friends James and Vince, who have always been quick to listen and slow to pass judgement.

When we honestly ask ourselves which person in our lives mean the most to us, we often find that it is those who, instead of giving advice, solutions, or cures, have chosen rather to share our pain and touch our wounds with a warm and tender hand. The friend who can be silent with us in a moment of despair or confusion, who can stay with us in an hour of grief and bereavement, who can tolerate not knowing, not curing, not healing and face with us the reality of our powerlessness, that is a friend who cares.

~ Henri Nouwen

A life is either all spiritual or not spiritual at all. No man can serve two masters. Your life is shaped by the end you live for. You are made in the image of what you desire.

~ THOMAS MERTON

CONTENTS

INTRODUCTION

*The most holy and important practice
in the spiritual life is the presence of
God - that is, every moment to take great
pleasure that God is with you.*
~ Brother Lawrence

This is my attempt to put into words the journey God has led me on during my life. My journey is not unique, others have traveled similar paths, but as God has uniquely made me, aspects of my path are uniquely mine.

God began leading me long before I came to Christ, through the work of many He brought into my life. I particularly remember an Episcopal Priest who served as the Head Master at St Christopher's, the school I attended from first through sixth grades in Lubbock, Texas. I have always had a profound inability to spell. During the 3rd grade, Mrs. Payne, my teacher, felt a visit to the Head Master was just what I needed each Friday after I failed my spelling test. What Mrs. Payne meant for punishment God worked for good. By the end of the year, I truly looked forward to my visits with him. I wish I could remember his name; to this day I can still clearly see his face. He took an interest in encouraging me, building into me spiritually, and through my failure, he had a profound influence on my life. In many regards, my deepest spiritual roots, through my poor spelling, are Episcopalian. Through my relationship with my friend and next door neighbor, Ret, and watching the impact of Christ on his family, I accepted Christ as my Lord and Savior when I turned fifteen. From then and for the next three decades, He led me down a road with considerable emphasis on knowledge and doctrine. In my 40's, He gave me a yearning for more, for something different, which is what this book is about. Ultimately, He led me to the more contemplative or mystical traditions of Christianity.

What do I mean by contemplative or mystical traditions?

The term contemplation or contemplative prayer has been described as, "prayer in which you experience God's presence within you, closer than breathing, closer than thinking, closer than consciousness itself." (Contemplative Outreach, n.d.) It is a stage of prayer characterized by deep listening. In contemplation you stop "doing" anything and are simply present to God. Gradually, God may become present to you, that is up to God. All you are doing is making yourself available to God. Contemplation is a letting go of doing, thinking, meditating, reflecting, or speaking. It is a focus on being "all ears" in an ambience of love, with God.

I think it is important to reiterate this point. Traditionally, contemplation or contemplative prayer, has been understood to be something that cannot be achieved through sheer effort of will. Rather it is God's gift, as you consent, simply to be in His presence, opening your heart, your whole being, to God. Contemplative prayer is a process of interior transformation. It is a relationship initiated by God and has the possibility of leading, if you consent, to divine union. We will delve into this more in the following chapters.

Please understand, I would not presumptuously say, "I have arrived and am in union with God". As I go further down this path, I often think I am further away from God than when I started, as He reveals the distance yet to travel. It is a journey more than a destination, but I believe it is a journey worth taking. During my journey, I have learned to be much more content with where God has me now, at this moment, knowing that He is with me, and leaving the end result to God.

My faith journey began in the Protestant tradition. In 1977, although a Christian for the past two years, I wasn't attending church regularly and decided for the most upright of reasons, that I needed to start! I chose my church tradition through the most rigorous of methods. Basically, I was madly in love with a girl,

Cindy, who later became my wife. She was attending a Bible Church, Midland Bible, which became the church I attended when visiting. Since I wanted to see her often, church became a bigger part of my life. Although not for the purest of motives, my journey towards God began with Bible Churches!

In 1979, after taking a four month sabbatical from college to sail from Florida to the Tongan Islands in the South Pacific, I was back in Lubbock, Texas, preparing to re-enter Texas Tech University in pre-med. Cindy was also attending Texas Tech that year, and I remember her coming and asking, "Do you want to go to a missions conference in Urbana, Illinois, with me and some others?" Through my testosterone driven mind, I translated this as, "Do you want to go on a trip with me for a week!" I really knew nothing about missions, but I did want to spend time with her! So, in early January 1980, I found myself in Urbana, Illinois, listening to Elisabeth Elliot and others, learning about missions. The book and movie, "End of the Spear", by Steve Saints, highlights Elisabeth Elliot and Steve Saints' father's stories.

Although I went because of Cindy, God worked on my heart ,and I heard His calling towards a life of missions, specifically medical missions. Of course, I still had 2 years of pre-med, 4 years of medical school, and 4 years of residency in front of me before I could consider a life of overseas missions. With Cindy, I later attended a Bill Gothard's Basic Youth Conflicts seminar, I met with Mike Halsey, the pastor at Midland Bible, many times, I attended a bible church in my home town, ...

Cindy and I were married in 1982 at Midland Bible Church. We then moved to Dallas, Texas, and I started medical school at Southwestern Medical School while Cindy worked as a clinical dietician. During our 8 years in Dallas, we attended Northwest Bible Church, studied through a Navigator's course, emphasizing scripture memorization, and began to grow in faith. In 1990, after finishing medical school and my residency at Parkland Hospital in obstetrics and gynecology, with two kids in tow, Eric and Catherine, we moved back to Midland, Texas, and once again attended Midland Bible. During my 10 years of training since that Urbana conference, that initial loud call I had heard from God to enter missions had become a quiet whisper. Over the next 15 years, God, through Midland Bible, with a strong emphasis on Bible knowledge and doctrine, helped me to grow spiritually. I would not have become who I am if not for those formative years.

By 2004, I had helped found a Christian Classical school, Midland Classical Academy, and had become an elder at Midland Bible. Despite all of this knowledge about God and work for God, I was also developing a growing longing in my heart I couldn't satisfy with either knowledge of God or doctrine. What I longed for was intimacy with God. A desire to see Him, "Face to Face". I also had not yet learned that this couldn't be fulfilled by doing things for God, through my own efforts.

As part of this journey, in 2002, returning to my desire to be involved in medical missions, I began serving on short term trips as a medical missionary in Russia. Why Russia? Basically, I had met the founder of Agape Unlimited, Bill Becknell, M.D., at a medical conference hosted by Focus On The Family. I was looking for opportunities to serve in missions. I went by Dr. Bill's booth at the conference several times, and he and I saw "eye to eye". I was looking for an opportunity to not just go and do medicine but to use medicine as a tool for sharing the Gospel. That was what Agape was doing in Russia. I told Dr. Bill, "I can go once!"

Since then, I have come to understand, "God has a sense of humor". Personally, I like the warmth, the tropics, and sailing. My personal ideal for missions would have involved medicine and a sailboat. Naturally, God sent me to Siberia! I did go "once", on my first trip in May 2002, with my son Eric. That first trip was hard and stretched me spiritually. I actually came home and told Cindy, "You won't have to worry about going to Russia as I won't be going back!" God worked on my heart though. I loved sharing the Gospel through my medical care, and I liked the challenge of working in the only ministry using medicine as a tool to share the Gospel in Russia, a country that spans 11 time zones, has over 180 different people groups with 79 still considered unreached, and that encompasses one eighth of the entire world's land mass! So, despite telling Cindy, "I won't be going back", I did go back on 4 more trips over the next 3 years.

In 2006, responding to that Call from long ago, I knew God wanted me to be more involved than just one to two trips per year. The challenge though was Russia was one country in which I wouldn't be able to fully practice medicine, and I didn't believe God was calling me to give up medicine. What to do? I trusted that God would provide an opportunity for me to at least practice medicine part-time, and I knew Agape needed someone who would be more involved by managing the ministry in the states. Through many sleepless nights, I thought by God's leading, my role would be to serve the ministry by dividing my time between the US, developing and overseeing the ministry, and Russia. Not knowing what the future held, I took a step of faith and turned in my resignation at Midland Women's Clinic, trusting God would provide a path forward. That path came through Midland Women's Clinic. Over the next decade, they gave me the opportunity to work part-time. In June 2006, not knowing what my patients would think, I stopped the obstetrical portion of my practice, focused solely on gynecology, and began dividing my time between Midland and Russia. Being gone long portions of the year wasn't conducive to good relationships with my pregnant patients who always wanted to deliver babies according to their schedule and not mine!

Since then, I have been serving with Agape Unlimited year-round, in Russia several months out of the year, flying back and forth 4-5 times yearly. I also continued serving as a board member at Midland Classical Academy until August 2013, and serving as an elder at Midland Bible until August 2015.   All this while maintaining a full-time medical practice, while in Midland. During much of this time, filled with knowledge of God, doing lots of things for God, I still felt this growing longing to see God "Face to Face".

During the early years spent working in Russia, although exciting and fun, there was also loneliness. We still had our youngest daughter, Rebecca, at home in junior high. Rebecca and Cindy would join me in Russia when schedules allowed, but many of the trips were alone. Traveling back and forth to Russia, I had one foot in two different cultures. I traveled from home to home, yet had no home. I belonged in both places yet didn't belong in either. I deeply longed for a deeper relationship with God, intimacy with God, yet had no guides. Since I was serving as an elder, a doctor, and a missionary, I felt I had few I could share my struggles with and found little help in the traditions of my Protestant faith. I began exploring teachers from the Russian Orthodox and Catholic faiths and learned about totally different perspectives on Christianity.

Thus begun, and lasting for several years, in the words of John of the Cross, began my "Dark night of the soul". (Dark Night of the Soul, n.d.)

One dark night,
fired with love's urgent longings
– ah, the sheer grace! –
I went out unseen,
my house being now all stilled.

In darkness, and secure,
by the secret ladder, disguised,
– ah, the sheer grace! –
in darkness and concealment,
my house being now all stilled.

On that glad night,
in secret, for no one saw me,
nor did I look at anything,
with no other light or guide
than the one that burned in my heart.

Over the next several years, I followed many rabbit trails with many blind holes. I also developed several friendships with others traveling a similar journey. I believe God took me down the path He had for me. Without the focus on doctrine and the focus on doing, I never would have had the hole that couldn't be filled by either, which ultimately led me to the

Contemplative path.

Over time, God has given me the desire of my heart. I do have a closer intimacy with Him and am more fully able to "pray without ceasing", i.e. seeing life through God's eyes as I go through my day. Certainly, I am not so presumptuous as to say I have arrived, but I believe I am on the path He has chosen for me and am content with the journey.

This book is my attempt to summarize the things I have found helpful, and the tools I use. Understand though, just as tools do not make a master carpenter, neither do tools create intimacy with God. A man becomes a carpenter through developing an intimacy with wood. Yes, tools are necessary for good carpentry, but they are only tools; they require the hands of a skilled carpenter to come to life. In the same way, spiritual disciplines are simply tools; they are not equal to intimacy with God. Yet, through the practice of spiritual disciplines, which I would call the contemplative path, God takes our use of them and our faltering efforts to foster intimacy with Him. This is also not meant to be a prescribed program. Everyone is unique, a unique image bearer of God. Thus, your relationship with God, which comprises two unique individuals, you and God, will be unique to you.

Nevertheless, I believe there is much to draw from in looking at the traditions that spring from the Desert Fathers and the monastic branch of our Christian heritage.

See what resonates with you and what you may be called to practice given where you are on your current path. Take the tools that work for you, realizing that just as you are unique, you will have a unique intimacy with God. I hope you find the tools useful. Don't grow weary. Intimacy with God, like intimacy with human relationships, takes time and effort and has refreshing times and dry spells.

God has me on the path of ultimate glorification, He is walking with me, He is in me, He is the core of my being, and He knows me better and more intimately than I know myself. So, I am content. Each day, I come to a fuller realization of the intimacy I already have with God, but that has not yet been fully realized by me because of my sin and weakness. Do I stumble and fail? Of course, I am human, but I am on the journey.

CHRISTIAN CONTEMPLATION AND A NEW MONASTICISM

'...the restoration of the church will surely come only from a new type of monasticism which has nothing in common with the old but a complete lack of compromise in a life lived in accordance with the Sermon on the Mount in the discipleship of Christ. I think it is time to gather people together to do this...' ~ Dietrich Bonhoeffer (January 14, 1935)

My journey towards the more mystical and monastic practices in Christianity began in earnest in the summer of 2008, while serving as a Protestant missionary in Russia working to reach many of the 180 different people groups living there. I had been serving since 2002 and seeking a deeper intimacy with God since 2004, but during that summer, I spent a day with and had lunch with the Holy Mother Olympics of the Khotkov Convent, founded in 1281, the oldest convent in Russia. What struck me is that although we were both Christian, we approached our faith in very different ways and thus had very different relationships with our Lord and Savior. A friend, a catholic priest, shared with me that one difference between the Orthodox, Catholics, and Protestants is that the Orthodox are drawn to the Gospel of John and mysticism, the Catholics to the Gospel of Matthew and hierarchy, and the Protestants to the Epistles and doctrine. Of course with any generalization, there are limitations. Nevertheless, I think this does, in a brief way, characterize some of the differences between these Christian traditions, the difference between me and the Holy Mother Olympics, and explain how we need each other in the broader community of believers.

That meeting led me down a path of deep learning concerning the Orthodox faith. My thought was that if I was going to minister to the Russian people, I really needed a deep understanding of the Orthodox faith. Studying Orthodoxy led me to a study of the great schism and the differences between Orthodoxy and Catholicism. This led me to a broader study of Catholicism.

Through my learning, the Orthodox Church has given me the spiritual wisdom of the Desert Fathers, found in the Philokalia, and the wisdom of Kallistos Ware; the Catholic Church has given me the wisdom and structure through their monastic institutions and such contemporary writers as Thomas Merton, Thomas Keating, Henri Nouwen, and others; and the Protestant Church served as the nursery for my spiritual birth with a heavy emphasis on doctrine. The Protestant Chuch is the church through which I first came to faith and it is my spiritual home. So, through my journey, as I worked to bring others to God, God through others, brought me more fully to Him.

Continuing this journey begun in 2008 and following a four-day retreat in 2018 to Mepkin Abbey, a monastery in South Carolina, which is part of the Cistercian or Trappist Order, I did an internet search on lay monastic life. I found many groups built around Third Order monasticism or New Monasticism that have sprung up literally around the world. So, what is Third Order monasticism and how does it relate to Christian Contemplation?

Monastic orders are predominantly found in the Orthodox and Catholic traditions, although some can also be found amongst the Anglican, Lutheran, and Episcopal in the Protestant faith. The First Order refers to men, the monks and friars, who most commonly live in a cloistered community together and strictly follow the tenets of the order. The Second Order refers to women, the nuns, who most often live in community and strictly follow the tenets, like the men. The Third Order, which has a rich history through the centuries, refers most often to priests, pastors, and lay men and women who choose, to the best of their ability, to follow the tenets of and be associated with a monastic order, but do not live in a cloistered community. They are secular in the sense of being engaged in the secular world by working and living in secular communities. They are involved with their local church, are often married, yet they strive to follow a more contemplative path and live according to the principles of the religious order with which they are affiliated. They do this while living in a much more hectic and secular life than what is found in a monastery or convent.

Following a third order, as a married man, a father and grandfather, working as a physician, serving in Russia, I will live life in a far different way than the men and women who commit their lives entirely to a monastic community. We will have similar but also unique contemplative paths.

◆ ◆ ◆

What is Christian Contemplation?

The Christian Contemplative Tradition is summarized below by Contemplative Outreach: (Christian Contemplative Tradition, n.d.)

> *Though it has acquired other meanings and connotations in recent centuries, the word contemplation had a specific meaning for the first 16 centuries of the Christian era. St. Gregory the Great summed up this meaning at the end of the 6th century as the knowledge of God that is impregnated with love. For Gregory, contem-*

*plation was both the fruit of reflecting on the
Word of God in scripture and a precious gift of
God. He referred to contemplation as "resting in
God." In this "resting," the mind and heart are
not so much seeking God, as beginning to experience what they have been seeking. This state is
not the suspension of all activity, but the reduc-
tion of many acts and reflections to a single act
or thought in order to sustain one's consent to
God's presence and action.*

Recent contemplative writers, following the traditions first developed by the Desert Fathers and later
cultivated in monastic communities, have outlined
three different layers of spiritual practice, which address bringing wholeness not only to the individual
but also address their role in their church community
and to their broader secular and social communities.
The first, inner practices, practicing Silence, allows us
to rest in the presence of God and experience inner
transformation. The second, prayer and church community practices, i.e. following the Liturgy of the
Hours, practicing sabbath, confession, community
worship, intercessory prayer, and seasonal reflection,
helps us focus on our role in the health of our church

community. The third, service or missional practices, are meant to help move society itself toward wholeness or shalom, meaning peace, harmony, and wholeness. These would include work toward inclusion, peace, justice, serving the poor, and hospitality.

As beginners on the contemplative path, we first must clean out the inside of the cup (Mt 23:26) or allow the inner transformation to take place through the unloading of the unconscious. Our initial focus then is on contemplative practices for the individual. Ultimately though, our goal is that this inner transformation radiates outward into all facets of life; the familial, communal, economic, and political spheres, to help open ourselves and our communities to shalom to the greatest extent possible.

Christian Contemplatives & Contemplative Practices Throughout History

Contemplative prayer is by no means a modern addition to Christianity. Contemplative Christian prayer has representatives in every age. A form of contemplative prayer was first practiced and taught by the Desert Fathers of Egypt, Palestine, and Syria including Evagrius, St. Augustine, and St. Gregory the Great in the West, and Pseudo-Dionysius and the Hesychasts in the East.

In the Middle Ages, St. Bernard of Clarivaux, William of St. Thierry, and Guigo the Carthusian, represent the Christian contemplative tradition, as well as the Rhineland mystics, including St. Hildegard, St. Mechtilde, Meister Eckhart, Ruysbroek, and Tauler. Later, the author of The Imitation of Christ and the English mystics of the 14th century such as the author of The Cloud of Unknowing, Walter Hilton, Richard Rolle, and Julian of Norwich, became part of the Christian contemplative heritage.

After the Reformation, the Carmelites of St. Teresa of Avila, St. John of the Cross, and St. Therese of Lisieux; the French school of spiritual writers, including St. Francis de Sales, St. Jane de Chantal, and Cardinal Berulle; the Jesuits, including fathers De Caussade, Lallemont, and Surin; the Benedictines, like Dom Augustine Baker, Dom John Chapman, and modern Cistercians such as Dom Vital Lehodey and Thomas Merton, all cultivated practices in their lives that they believed led to the spiritual gift of contemplation.

In the 20th and 21st centuries, initiatives have been taken by various religious orders, predominantly in the Catholic, Anglican, and Episcopal faiths, to renew the contemplative orientation of their founders and to share their spirituality with laypeople. Several Catholic monks, such as Fathers Thomas Keating and John Main, have pioneered efforts to return contemplative practices to a broader audience in Christian spirituality. The product of these initiatives is a myriad of modern prayer practices based on historical contemplative teachings.

Modern Contemplative Practices

Prayer of Faith, Prayer of the Heart, Pure Prayer, Prayer of Simplicity, Prayer of Simple Regard, Active Recollection, Active Quiet, and Acquired Contemplation are all names of modern practices based on historical practices and meant to lead their practitioners to contemplation. Two such practices, Centering Prayer and Lectio Divina, are closely derived from ancient contemplative Christian practices and are attempts to present these practices in updated formats that appeal to the lay community. We will explore these two practices in subsequent chapters.

As a rule of life, I love this quote from Corine Ware's book, "Saint Benedict on the Freeway, A Rule of Life for the 21st Century", concerning contemplative practices:

> *Most of us unconsciously follow some sort of daily routine, even though we may not think of it as a rule. We like the security of feeling that after we have done this, followed by that, and then there is one other thing ... A Rule of Life, as the ancients called it, is a pattern of daily actions chosen to accomplish something. The goal of a Rule is recollection ... the continuous remembrance of God.*

We often perceive that rules limit our freedom and even the word 'rule' can have a bad connotation. The 'rule' about which we speak in contemplative practices doesn't have to do with harmful limitation, this Rule is about freedom. How freeing would it be if we felt ourselves to always be in God's presence! Imagine what a difference such a sense of God's accompanying Presence could make.

People who are often the most influential decide what is most important in their lives and eliminate anything that does not directly contribute to their chosen goal. An example is Benjamin Franklin. In his autobiography, he says that at one time he constructed for himself what he calls a 'liturgy,' for his daily private use. He listed all the virtues he wished for himself: temperance, silence, order, frugality, industry; in all, a total of 13. He set about to keep these by making a little book in which, he says, 'I allotted a page for each of the virtues.' A grid was drawn on each page so that the week's progress could be recorded. As to his daily rule, he chose to ask himself one question each morning: 'What good shall I do this day?' Again, in the evening, he called himself to account with the question, 'What good have I done today?'

We may not be as obsessive as Franklin, making a written record of each day's progress, although it is very similar to Ignatius' Daily Examen discussed later in the book, but if the goal of our life is companionship with God, constructing first and following a Rule of Life aimed to accomplish that end can be a great place to start! Of course, simply following the rule doesn't guarantee intimacy with God. All we are doing by following the rule is fostering and communicating with God our desire for intimacy, our availability. Actual intimacy is the work of God in our hearts through the Holy Spirit.

Repetition and association are key to a sustained spiritual life. Intermittent inspirational moments, such as my time at the missions conference long ago, have their important place and are the initial reason most of us seek the 'something more'. But finally, it is in learning to work out our spiritual life in our daily common life where we find our deepest growth.

There are those who have gone before us who also believed in the value of regularity for sustained religious life. They worked out daily patterns of prayer that may be useful to us. (Ware)

For me, as I look at third order monasticism, the order I am most drawn to is the Third Order of St Francis. Simon Tugwell defines spirituality as 'a way of looking at the world', and Franciscan spirituality as 'a way of radical unprotectedness'. That is about as apt a definition as it is possible to give. Francis was in love with God and threw himself into the love relationship with the dangerous abandon of a lover. Certainly, I am not there, but I can't imagine a better goal to strive for!

As you look through the principles we will discuss, trying to figure out what to adapt to your life, I think the overarching guiding principle can be found in Philippians 2:12-13

Work out your own salvation with fear and trembling, for it is God who works in you, both to will and to work for His good pleasure.

Quotes

I encourage you, then, to make experience, not knowledge, your aim. Knowledge often leads to arrogance, but this humble feeling never lies to you. — (Anonymous)

◆ ◆ ◆

In meditation, we move beyond doctrines and dogmas to inner experience. ... When I am faithful to meditation, I quickly overcome the illusion that my correct thinking, or thinking more about something, can ever get me there. If that were so, every good PhD would be a saint!

You see, information is not the same as transformation. Even good and correct thinking is trapped inside my little mind, my particular cul-

ture, my form of education, my parental conditioning—all of which are good and all of which are bad. ... How could the Infinite ever be fully or rightly received by the mere finite? (Rohr, 2018)

"The monk's ultimate goal is direct union with the Godhead. But to aim at that goal is to miss it altogether. His task is to rid himself of ego so that consciousness, once its usual discordant mental content is dumped out of it through ritual prayer and meditation, may experience non-self as a living formlessness and emptiness into which God may come, if it please Him to come." *(Miller Jr.)*

"We often conceive of worldly life as merely a kind of default existence that anyone who is not specially called to monasticism or ordination simply ends up leading. We assume that it is only the monk, nun, or priest who has a special call, while the married woman, for instance, has merely been passed by. ... But we must not allow ourselves to approach it merely in these terms. Instead, every one of us should, indeed must, treat lay life as a calling just the way we think of monasticism and ordination. We must sit down with ourselves and with God in prayer to discern

if life in the world really is what we are meant for, and if we discover that it is, we must heed this call with the same seriousness with which we would treat a call to a hermit's life in the desert. (Opperwall)

PRINCIPLES OF THIRD ORDER LIVING

Loving God and loving one's neighbor are really the same thing. ~ Brother Lawrence

> *Contemplation is very far from being just one kind of thing that Christians do: it is the key to prayer, liturgy, art and ethics, the key to the essence of a renewed humanity that is capable of seeing the world and other subjects in the world with freedom—freedom from self-oriented, acquisitive habits and the distorted understanding that comes from them. To put it boldly, contemplation is the only ultimate answer to the unreal and insane world that our financial systems and our advertising culture and our chaotic and unexamined emotions encourage us to inhabit. To learn contemplative practice is to learn what we need so as to live truthfully and honestly and lovingly. It is a deeply revolutionary matter. (Williams, 2012)*

Each monastic order has its own unique approach towards fostering a contemplative life with their own unique set of rules and way of life. Even so, there are several principles that transcend all orders. The principles below, are described from the order of St. Benedict's Cistercian branch, but are also applicable across all Third Orders of the Christian faith.

Cultivate Silence

St. Benedict wrote, "Speaking and teaching are the master's task; the disciple is to be silent and listen" (RB 6:8). Silence is the environment that allows you to properly listen to God's voice and the voices of those God brings into your life. Often, we are uncomfortable with silence, even in church, we find it awkward with moments for silent reflection often only lasting a few seconds. So, we fill our days with needless noise and distractions. Turn off the music, especially in the car, moderate television and internet use. This will challenge you to listen to God who dwells within you and speaks in the depth of your heart. Additionally, being silent helps you to avoid the sins of gossip or detraction and possibly hear God through others. Often with others, our desire is not to listen but simply to share our thoughts. St. Benedict echoed the wisdom found in the Book of Proverbs which says, "In a flood of words you will not avoid sin," (RB 6:11). By avoiding unnecessary noise in your life, you will learn to cultivate inner silence, which is the ideal setting for prayer and intimacy with God.

Ideas for Cultivating Silence

Centering Prayer

Grand Silence

Silent Retreat

Find ways to extend Silence into your normal day

Be Faithful to Daily Prayer

St. Benedict said, "Prayer should, therefore, be short and pure, unless perhaps it is prolonged under the inspiration of divine grace" (RB 20:4). This instruction is comforting for those of us who have a demanding work week, hectic schedule, and are burdened with numerous responsibilities at home. We may not be able to dedicate large blocks of time to prayer, nevertheless, we should find time in the morning to praise God before each day begins and pray in thanksgiving during the evening before going to bed. One option is to pray the Liturgy of the Hours to sanctify the day, specifically being faithful to Morning and Evening Prayer. Whatever your practice, you want to develop a heartfelt attitude to God while you are praying, offering yourself and your loved ones into God's care. Many opportunities will arise throughout the day to offer brief prayers of trust in God. The aim of monks, and all Christians, is to pray without ceasing. For me this term "pray without ceasing" has little to do with using actual words but pertains to keeping the memory of God alive in my heart and mind at every moment and in every situation.

Ideas for Cultivating Daily Prayer

Practice the Liturgy of the Hours at least 2 x daily

Intercessory Prayer

Jesus Prayer

Welcoming Prayer

Meditate on Scripture

The ancient monastic practice of Lectio Divina or "sacred reading" emphasizes a slow, prayerful reading of Scripture that is intended to allow you to listen to the Word and seek peace in God's presence. St. Benedict warned his monks, "Idleness is the enemy of the soul. Therefore, the brothers should have specified periods for manual labor as well as for prayerful reading" (RB 48:1). Contemplation on God's Word or other books of wisdom, if done reflectively and prayerfully, has the power of calling you to a continual conversion of life. Familiarize yourself with the method. Take between 15-30 minutes a day in a quiet environment to practice Lectio Divina with Scripture, the writings of the saints from the Philokalia (discussed later in this book), or other great spiritual works. Spiritual reading nourishes your mind and soul and often provides those inspired words that you need to hear and carry throughout the day. Encountering the Word of God each day and reflecting on it throughout the day, draws us into deeper communion with the One who speaks the word to us.

Ideas for Scripture Meditation

Practice Lectio Divina Meditation

Gospel Meditation

Scripture memorization

Practice Humility

Numerous passages from the Rule of St. Benedict stress the importance of humility. Particularly in Chapter 7, St. Benedict depicts humility as a ladder with twelve rungs which the monk is to ascend. The first step is that a monk should keep the "fear of God" always before his eyes (RB 7:10). When you fear God or are in "awe" of God, you maintain a right relationship, realizing that you are a creature and not God. Humility is a virtue that needs to be developed, and it entails being down to earth, honest, and truthful, in prayer, at work, and in everyday matters. St. Benedict wrote, "*Place your hope in God alone. If you notice something good in yourself, give credit to God, not to yourself, but be certain that the evil you commit is always your own and yours to acknowledge*" (RB 4:41-43). Being a humble person means being grateful for the blessings and opportunities that God gives you and recognizing that your gifts and talents have God as their source. Allow daily struggles, and even falling into sin, to be an invitation to humility. Admit without hesitation that you must depend entirely on God's grace, and not on your strength. I like this quote from Teresa of Avila, "The Interior Castle":

You can become overly concerned about yourself. This

is a fine point you must not miss if you would continue to grow in spirit: the moment you focus on yourself again, you place yourself in the center of your attentions and not the Lord! . . . Do not dwell upon your inner failings . . . Instead, merely accept the fact that you are an easily failing creature.

Ideas for Cultivating Humility

Practice Ignatius' Daily Examen

Simplicity of Living

Self-Denial

Deep Listening to others

Form Authentic Community

Monks support and encourage one another in their community. They particularly encourage those encountering difficulties, and they celebrate with one another during joyful times. St. Benedict instructed, "No one is to pursue what he judges better for himself, but instead, what he judges better for someone else. To their fellow monks, they show the pure love of brothers" (RB 72:7-8). In a world of individualism, social media and superficial relationships, all people long for a deep sense of belonging and communion with one another. The spiritual life is always a journey that we undertake with others. You must be willing to invest the time and energy to engage personally with other people and have a genuine interest in their lives. Allow your conversations to pass from surface level topics to the more meaningful areas of life. You should gather with others who share your faith, values, and desire for God. Praying together, reading and discussing a spiritual book and Bible studies are all ways of coming together to grow in faith.

Ideas for Forming Authentic Community

Practice Hospitality

Practice your vocation as unto the Lord

Be involved in your local church

Behold others and nature

Volunteer in your community, particularly in serving the poor

Find other like-minded people for encouragement along the path

Tree of Contemplative Practices

The tree of contemplative practices, from contemplativemind.org, builds on this image of a tree representing a contemplative life and is a good illustration for showing how the different principles in the Third Order relate to each other to provide a full contemplative life. As we work to develop our own contemplative tree, the roots symbolize the two intentions that are the foundation of all contemplative practices: cultivating awareness of God in each moment and developing a stronger connection to God, the Trinity, and to one another. (Contemplative Tree, n.d.)

The branches represent the different groupings of practices. For example, *Stillness* practices focus on quieting the mind and body in order to develop calmness and focus. *Generative* practices come in many different forms Lectio Divina, beholding beauty in nature and others, chanting, but share the common intent of generating thoughts and feelings of devotion and compassion, rather than calming and quieting the mind. The *Activist and Relational* practices are about fostering community through acts of service, deep listening to others, storytelling. Other branches include: *Creative* practices; art, music, journaling and reflect that we are born in God's image as creative beings. *Ritual* practices; liturgy, liturgical calendars, rites of passage, and retreats, foster community by means of corporate worship, celebrating milestones in life and finding ways to bond together. *Movement* practices; yoga, walking meditation, hikes, reflect that we are physical beings and incorporate our body and movement into contemplation.

Indeed, all of life's activities are a contemplative practice and can be included on this Tree. This includes the parts of life we often don't think of as being spiritual: cooking, cleaning, eating, grooming, … These can all become spiritual when done with the intent of cultivating awareness or developing a stronger connection with God or one's inner wisdom. Find the practices that speak to you on each of the branches and add your own branches, such as *Humility* (Simplicity, Hospitality, …) or *Work,* to create your own full contemplative tree.

Another example of a tree as an illustration of a contemplative life is a bonsai tree. In Japanese culture, a bonsai tree is representative of peace, balance and harmony. They are representative of all that is good and correct with the world.

Bonsai trees in particular play a large role in the symbolism of life. They are often associated with simplicity and the beauty that simple things can provide. Bonsai trees are manipulated by their gardener to form balance, simplicity, and harmony and the older a bonsai tree is, often the more beautiful it becomes.

Most criticisms I hear concerning contemplation tend to focus on a single aspect of contemplation, most commonly silence. Imagine your own contemplative or Bonsai tree if you put all of your contemplative energy into a single branch, a single practice, allowing the others to wither and die. Your tree would appear distorted, unbalanced. Indeed, with a full, balanced contemplative tree, we can see that contemplation is not only about stillness and silence, but also relationship and activity. It becomes much less about what we do but our attitude and perspective while we do what God calls us to do.

CULTIVATE SILENCE

Silence is God's First Language
~ John of the Cross

In the night of sense, God is feeding us from within rather than engaging our faculties through the external senses, memory, imagination, and reason. In contemplative prayer these faculties are at rest so that our intuitive faculties, the passive intellect, and the will-to-God, may access the 'still point,' the place where our personal identity is rooted in God as an abiding presence. The divine presence has always been with us, but we think it is absent. That thought is the monumental illusion of the human condition. The spiritual journey is designed to heal it. ... Silence is God's first language; everything else is a poor translation. In order to hear that language, we must learn to be still and to rest in God. (Keating)

THE ENORMITY OF LIFE'S tasks weighs and press on the day ... they demand and insist on a constancy of attention that is relentless. Ah ... but we are fortunate to have night's solace—in the silence that is created by the dark.

Night ... that melancholy time, when the stars remind us of the silence of God. Here we can remember the future, and lean into the unknown, setting aside the oppressive weight of our carefully constructed version of who we think we are, and release that side of the pool. We can remember how to see in the dark ... with our ears ... This silence sends us on a different pilgrimage. It guards the heart's fire and teaches us to speak from within, with a language that is imbued with the sacred. Words thus nurtured in this holy silence fly forth with the wings of joy and return to lead us back to the silence from which they were born. (Sanders-Sardello)

It is time to rediscover the true order of priorities. As expressed by Martin Laird in Into the Silent Land, "It is precisely this noisy chaotic mind that keeps us ignorant of the deeper reality of God as the ground of our being. This ignorance is pervasive and renders us like the proverbial deep-sea fisherman, who spends his life fishing for minnows while standing on a whale". (Silence is Gods First Language, n.d.)

◆ ◆ ◆

Silence is more important than any other human work. Because it expresses God. The true revolution comes from silence; it leads us toward God and toward others so that we can place ourselves humbly at their service. (Sarah, 2017)

◆ ◆ ◆

Centering Prayer

Forget everything but God and fix on Him your naked desire, your longing stripped of all self-interest.
~ The Cloud of Unknowing

As we discussed in chapter one, Prayer of Faith, Prayer of the Heart, Pure Prayer, Prayer of Simplicity, Prayer of Simple Regard, Active Recollection, Active Quiet, and Acquired Contemplation are all names of modern practices based on historical practices and meant to lead their practitioners to contemplation. Two such practices, Centering Prayer and Lectio Divina, are closely derived from ancient contemplative Christian practices and are attempts to present these practices in updated formats that appeal to the lay community.

In this chapter, I would like to narrow the scope of the discussion on contemplative, silent prayer to the discipline of Centering Prayer, although all of the disciplines mentioned above, have a similar goal of fostering silence and simply being before God.

> *The discipline of Centering Prayer . . . is a way of refining our receptive apparatus so that we can perceive the word of God communicating itself with ever greater simplicity to our spirit and to our inmost being. . .. The Spirit's gifts of wisdom and understanding become more powerful . . . enabling us to rest in the presence of God. ... Waiting on God strengthens our capacity for interior silence and makes us sensitive to the delicate movements of the Spirit in daily life that lead to purification and holiness. ~ Intimacy with God*

Centering Prayer is a method of silent prayer developed by Thomas Keating and others as a means of bringing the contemplative life they lived as monks in their monastic communities to a modern, non-monastic audience. Based on the 13th century English devotional classic *The Cloud of Unknowing*, it lays the inner groundwork for entering Contemplative Prayer and builds upon the foundation laid by the Desert Fathers, who lived in isolation. The silence we cultivate during this time is a consent to God's presence and action within, a God who is nearer than our very breath. It is not intended as a replacement for regular prayer practices, but to provide a deepening and expansive context for them.

Centering Prayer is also based on the wisdom saying of Jesus in the Sermon on the Mount (Matthew 6:6): "If you want to pray, enter your inner room, close the door and pray to your Father in secret, and your Father who sees in secret will reward you."

A Simple Outline of Centering Prayer

The steps mentioned below are guidelines. The fruit of this prayer is not something you produce. You simply reduce the obstacles by providing an interior environment in which the Spirit can speak without words in the inmost depths of your being.

The first step in Centering Prayer is to enter your inner room, which is symbolized by the heart in most traditions; that is, your innermost self beyond the senses and beyond thinking. Choose a word or short phrase, which may or may not be sacred, as a symbol of your intention to consent to God's presence and action within. The word should be short and not emotionally charged to limit mental distractions. A few examples are God, Lord, Jesus, Father, Abba, Be Still, Be Near Me, Love, Agape, Peace, Stillness, Mercy, ... The sacred word is sacred not because of its inherent meaning, but because of the meaning you give it as the expression of your intention and consent.

Although Centering Prayer focuses on using a word, other contemplative prayer methods recommend focusing on your breath or using a sacred image to focus your gaze on. No matter which symbol you choose, word, breath, or image, remember that the symbol does not establish you in interior silence; it is simply to reaffirm your original intention to be in God's presence and to be open to the divine action by helping to redirect you away from the inevitable thoughts, worries, inspirations, that will come.

> *Let this little word represent God in all his fullness and nothing less than the fullness of God. Let nothing except God hold sway in your mind and heart.*

~ The Cloud of Unknowing

Second, "close the door," symbolizing your intention of letting go of all thoughts, preoccupations, memories and plans during this time. Sit comfortably, upright, in a relaxed position in a chair or utilizing a prayer bench, usually with eyes closed. Keep the back straight, let go of all thought, and gently introduce your sacred word, focus on your breath, or gaze upon or mentally recall the image you have chosen as the symbol of your consent to God's presence and action within.

Inevitably, you will be overtaken by thoughts, emotions, images, memories, an itchy nose, or other sensation. In short, any distraction. Return to your original intention to let go of all thinking by gently returning to your sacred symbol to help release the distraction. It is also important once you have chosen a symbol to stay with that symbol for a season, let not only the prayer but also the symbol work within you. In particular, don't change symbols during your prayer time as changing your symbol during prayer can be its own distraction!

Don't be discouraged if you find yourself swinging from pleasant experiences, to emotionally charged experiences, to flashes of inspiration, to boredom. Each is a distraction. Particularly with emotions, part of the unfolding process is an unloading or identifying and releasing some of the pain we accumulate and store in our unconscious. Also, don't be surprised if thoughts seem to come up quicker than you can let them go. Just remember to return to your symbol, your intention of letting go, and being before and with God. Thomas Keating shared a story about teaching this method to a nun. The nun said, "O Thomas, I am terrible at this, in twenty minutes I must have had ten thousand thoughts enter my mind!" Thomas replied, "Wonderful! Ten thousand opportunities to return to God!"

At the end of the prayer period, remain in silence for a few minutes to transition back to your ordinary flow of consciousness. It may help to have a transitional practice, like reciting a Psalm, a verse, or the Jesus Prayer.

The recommended time for Centering prayer is fifteen to twenty minutes twice a day. I find it helpful to use a meditation app on my phone, such as Timeless, as a timer so that I don't become distracted by wondering how long I have been in prayer and how long before I'm done. The purpose of the practice is not radical change during the time of prayer itself, but to just practice consenting to be open to God's presence. Often though, this practice of consenting in silence is carried into the rest of the day by fostering an on-going sense of God's presence throughout the day.

The goal of the practice is not found in the quality of the silence you are trying to produce, it is found simply through the willingness to rest in God's presence, despite what might come up in your mind. This practice is a simple means of cultivating a deepening intimacy with the God who is always already present.

The source of Centering Prayer then is not some aspiration, expectation, or far off ideal, but rather its source is the transcendent reality of the divine life present within you right now. When you are sitting in Centering Prayer, you may seem to be doing nothing, you may think of it as a waste of time. But, you are doing perhaps the most important of all functions, which is to become who you are, the unique manifestation of the Word of God that the Spirit designed you to be... and to experience ever increasing interior freedom. ~ Intimacy with God

One final thought on Centering Prayer and possible dry seasons of prayer:

Suppose your meditation takes you to the point where you are baffled and repelled by the cloud that surrounds God? ... Far from realizing him, you begin to realize nothing more than your own helplessness to know him, and you begin to think that meditation is something altogether hopeless and impossible. And yet the more helpless you are, the more you seem to desire to see him and to know him.

The tension between your desires and your failure generates in you a painful longing for God which nothing seems able to satisfy. Do you think your meditation has failed? On the contrary: this bafflement, this darkness, this anguish of helpless desire is a fulfillment of meditation. For if meditation aims above all at establishing in your soul a vital contact of love with the living God, then as long as it only produces images and ideas and affections that you can understand, feel and appreciate, it is not yet doing its full quota of work. But when it gets beyond the level of your understanding... it is really bringing you close to God. (Merton)

❖ ❖ ❖

Grand Silence

In a monastic community, Grand Silence refers to the time that begins with the last prayer service of the day called Compline, usually around 8PM, and ends with the first prayer service the following morning, usually around 7AM. In chapter 42 of the Rule of St. Benedict it says, "Monks should diligently cultivate silence at all times, but especially at night." "When all have assembled, they should pray Compline; and on leaving Compline, no one will be permitted to speak further... except on occasions when guests require attention, or the abbot wishes to give someone a command, but even this is to be done with the utmost seriousness and proper restraint." Benedict speaks of the benefit of silence in chapter 6 where he cites several Scriptures on the vulnerability to sin that speaking produces. *(Prov. 10:19 and 18:21)* (Grand Silence, n.d.)

Think of silence as a form of fasting from speech, noise, distraction and all that go with them. Often in Scripture silence is the result of being confronted with our sin. Keeping silence before God is an expression of humility and submission and is a form of "Deep Listening" to God. Ultimately, we come before God, who is all knowing, all powerful, and present everywhere. As Habakkuk said, "The Lord is in his holy temple. Let all the earth keep silence before Him." Consider practicing Grand Silence at least 1-2 x monthly.

The Trinity delights in our words of praise. But because God is infinite, our understanding of Him will never fully capture the boundless truth about Him. Therefore, when contemplating on the greatness of God, keeping silence before him is an appropriate act of worship. It is an expression of holy awe.

Observing silence at night is a good time to recall and reflect on our day or on our lives. Monks were encouraged, in the quiet of night, to contemplate their deaths. By doing so, they identified ways their lives needed to change before that final day. They could also reflect upon the joy they will experience when they will one day be in the presence of God. This is where practicing the Examen, discussed in a later chapter, can be helpful.

Grand Silence is about being with Jesus. It is another way to practice Sabbath, to stop, to cease all our work, worry, or the whirlwind of activity and depend totally upon the Lord. It is a time for us to let go of all distractions. But letting go and moving to a point of internal stillness and silence takes time. We lead busy, full lives sometimes way beyond the margins of health and sanity. So be patient as you embrace the silence and receive it as a friend.

Etiquette for Silence in Community

Turn off your cell phone, your computer, and put down your novel for the evening. Rest in Jesus. If the computer or phone is a problem, give it to someone else for the night.

If you have difficulty settling, go for a walk with Jesus, draw, read Scripture, or if very tired, go to bed early.

If rooming with another, have a brief conversation about the morning routine so you won't be wondering who will do what when.

Honor the silence when entering common spaces.

In a group, many consider it best to keep your eyes down to avoid requiring a recognition or response from others. During meals you can focus your eyes on the edge of your plate.

As always, any discipline is subject to the command to love. If it is loving for you to break silence for another's benefit, feel free to do so.

During breakfast, think of Jesus as your meal mate, eating across from you. What would you like to talk with him about given this opportunity?

If you need to exercise in the morning, think of Jesus exercising with you. There is no need to talk. Just enjoy the time with God.

◆ ◆ ◆

Silent Retreat

Once or twice a year, consider attending a silent retreat, spending time at a monastery, or creating your own stay at home 1-2-day silent retreat. During the retreat, the time of silence of the Grand Silence practice can be extended to one or more days. At Mepkin Abbey, the monks have a monthly practice which they call "Desert Days" during which the monks observe 24 hours of silence, each retreating to their own area on the abbey property for an extended time of silence with God.

◆ ◆ ◆

Walking Contemplation

This practice helps us keep our awareness in the present moment. For many, the act of walking and maintaining fluid motion helps them stay attentive and alert in the present. Set aside a specific time to walk, roughly twenty minutes, with no phones or music to distract you, and pay attention to the quality of your awareness. Begin by standing still and taking several slow diaphragm breaths. Follow the breath in and out, then begin walking. As you walk, gently let thoughts go as they come up, like in Centering Prayer. Keep your awareness focused on the act of walking, how it feels in different areas of your body, the heels, the soles, the legs, the lungs, the arms. Notice colors and sense impressions on the external level but stay attentive to the interior space at the same time. Try not to get caught up in thoughts, labels, or mental stories. Notice the rhythm of movement and bring your awareness back to the body when thoughts come up. When you become aware of inner tension, recognize it, and let it go. You may need to slow your speed as you go and recognize you are there simply to enjoy the experience of being a body in motion.

BE FAITHFUL TO DAILY PRAYER

*Prayer is not just one of the many things
people do in their life, but rather the
basic receptive attitude out of which all
of life can receive new vitality.*

Liturgy of the Hours

In the morning I offer myself to You in prayer.
By night I surrender to You in trust.
O, that I might walk in the Light
with a grateful heart,
and radiate peace
to the world!

(Merrill)

While visiting Istanbul in 2014, Cindy and I stayed in a Best Western Hotel, just down the hill from the Blue Mosque and the Hagia Sophia. The Best Western, at a very reasonable cost, was probably one of the nicest hotels I have ever stayed in. We were on the top floor with two balconies, one overlooking both the Blue Mosque and the Hagia Sophia and the other overlooking the Bosporus Strait.

One of my fondest memories of that trip was hearing the "Adhan", the Islamic call to prayer, recited by the muezzin from the minarets of each mosque in the city, five times a day. The prayers could be heard while we were in our room, particularly early in the morning and in the evening, and while touring the city. In Islam, one of the five pillars of faith is the daily participation in Salat, or the five daily prayers. These consist of "Fajr", the dawn prayer, "Dhuhr", the early afternoon prayer, "Asr", the late afternoon prayer, "Maghrib", the sunset prayer, and "Isha'a", the night prayer. What I appreciated about the Salat was this constant reminder for the individual and for the community to stop the normal activities of life: work, commerce, cooking, cleaning, ... and pause to remember God. For most in Istanbul, it was an on-going reminder of Alah and to keep him present in their life. As I spent my time in Istanbul, it was hard not to participate, at least internally, in this fixed hour prayer and stop to remember the Trinity. Does Christianity have such a tradition? Certainly, in my Protestant roots it is hard to find, but it does have a rich tradition in our Catholic, Orthodox, and Anglican roots!

Fixed-hour prayer is one of the oldest Christian spiritual disciplines and has its roots in the Judaism out of which Christianity came. When the Psalmist says, "Seven times a day do I praise You," he is referring to fixed-hour prayer as it existed in ancient Judaism. We don't know the hours of prayer that were

67

appointed in the Psalmist's time, but by the time of Christ, the devout had come to punctuate their work day with prayers on a regimen that followed the flow of Roman commercial life. Forum bells began the work day at six in the morning, "prime" or first hour; sounded mid-morning break at nine, "terce" or third hour; the noon meal and siesta or break at twelve "sext" or sixth hour; the re-commencing of trade at three "none" or ninth hour; and the close of business at six "vespers". With the addition of evening prayers and early prayers upon arising, the structure of fixed-hour prayer was established in a form that is still used by Christians today.

Fixed-hour prayer is also commonly referred to as "The Divine Offices" or "the Liturgy of the Hours," and is found in various forms in the Orthodox, Roman Catholic, and Anglican Christian practices. Because of its long and elaborate history within Orthodox and Catholic Christianity, the hours have been most often observed by monastics and clergy rather than by laity. Why is this so? As we look at the prayers, we find that keeping the hours has developed into using a cumbersome number of books and assists and that they have often been chanted instead of spoken. Chanting is a rich custom that is not a necessity for participating in the prayers.

During my time at Mepkin Abbey, we used four different books at each liturgy and I found myself as a new participant becoming lost in the flipping between the many books. So, for one not reared within the Orthodox, Catholic, or Anglican traditions, the chanting of the prayers and the use of the cumbersome "books of hours" or breviary volumes forms an obstacle that can prove daunting to overcome.

This leads many to conclude that the Liturgy of the Hours is complicated and doesn't fit into their secular life. Who wants to carry the many volumes needed and who has time to participate with many of the sessions lasting twenty minutes or more? This need not be the case. I hope as we look further at the Liturgy of the Hours you will see that there is a way of fitting this practice into a hectic, secular life!

So, what is the Liturgy of the Hours? They are a meditative dialogue on the mystery of Christ, using scripture and prayer. At times the dialogue is between the Church or individual soul and God; at times it is even between the Church and the world. The dialogue is always held; however, in the presence of God and using the words and wisdom of God. Each of the seven Hours includes selections from the Psalms that culminate in a scriptural proclamation. The two most important or hinge Hours are Morning and Evening Prayer. (Liturgy of the Hours, n.d.)

Morning Prayer

> *Morning Prayer is a time of praise, a time of rising with Christ, the coming of the Risen Lord into our day, our life.*

Morning Prayer is intended and arranged to sanctify the morning. St. Basil the Great gives an excellent description of this: "It is said in the morning in order that the first stirrings of our mind and will may be consecrated to God and that we may take nothing in hand until we have been gladdened by the thought of God, as it is written: 'I was mindful of God and was glad' (Ps 77:4 [Jerome's translation from Hebrew]), or set our bodies to any task before we do what has been said: 'I will pray to you, Lord, you will hear my voice in the morning; I will stand before you in the morning and gaze on you' (Ps 5:4-5)."

Celebrated as the light of a new day is dawning,

this hour also recalls the resurrection of the Lord Jesus, the true light enlightening all people (see Jn 1:9) and "the sun of justice" (Mal 4:2), "rising from on high" (Lk 1:78). We can well understand the advice of St. Cyprian: "There should be prayer in the morning so that the resurrection of the Lord may thus be celebrated" (GILH, no. 38).

Daytime Prayer

Daytime Prayer is to be prayed at Midmorning, Noon, and Midafternoon.

> *Now is time for a break ... to pause, remember one's True Self, one's intention for the day, and the ever-present eye of God.*
>
> *It is now noon. As food is served, you can silently thank God and remember the world. It will not be much of a stretch, as you look at your plate, to realize that you have food before you and many in the world are in need. It is much more important to make this small remembrance than to despair, thinking that there is no way you can help... Your compassionate energy is made available to God in order to affect healing and help.*

No, this small moment is not a waste of time,
or an unimportant 'hour.' ~Corinne Ware, Saint
Benedict on the Freeway, A Rule of Life for the
21st Century

Liturgical custom in both the Orthodox and Catholic faiths have retained midmorning, midday, and midafternoon prayer, mainly because these hours were linked to a commemoration of the events of the Lord's passion and of the first preaching of the Gospel" (GILH, no. 74-75).

Often, praying three times a day, in the middle of the work day, may not fit into our daily schedule. A good compromise can be to pick one time, midmorning, noon, or midafternoon, depending upon your schedule, and make this a part of your routine.

Evening Prayer

Evening is approaching and the day is already
far spent.

Evening prayer is celebrated as a reflection on the day in order that we may give thanks for what has been given us today, or what we have done well during the day. Through evening prayer we can also recall God's redemption by interpreting it as a remembrance of Jesus' true evening sacrifices when He entrusted to the apostles at supper the mysteries of the Church and instituted the Eucharist or Communion. It can also be viewed as a remembrance of His evening sacrifice the next day when He offered Himself to the Father for the salvation of the whole world.

Night Prayer

Lord, now let your servant go in peace;
your word has been fulfilled:
my own eyes have seen the salvation
which you have prepared in the
sight of every people:
a light to reveal you to the nations
and the glory of your people Israel.
Glory to the Father
and to the Son
and to the Holy Spirit,
as it was in the beginning, is now,
and will be forever.
Amen.
Canticle of Simeon, Luke 2:29-32

Night prayer is the last prayer of the day, said before retiring, even if that is after midnight. (GILH, no. 84). Many early Christians viewed sleep as a form of death and thus a time to reflect upon our own ultimate death when we come to face our Lord. With this symbolism, the Psalms that are chosen for Night Prayer are full of confidence in the Lord. For Night Prayer, I like this quote from Dietrich Bonhoeffer.

"Darkness is upon us. The ancients had a sense of man's helplessness while sleeping, of the kinship of sleep with death. So, they prayed for the protection of the holy angels. Most remarkable and profound is the ancient prayer that when our eyes are closed in sleep, God may nevertheless keep our hearts awake. It is the prayer that God may dwell with us and in us even though we are unconscious of His presence, that He may keep our hearts pure and holy despite all the cares and temptations of the night, to make our hearts ever alert to hear His call. Even in sleep we are in the hands of God. Even in sleep God can perform His wonders upon us." (Bonhoeffer)

Resources Available

As we have seen, the Liturgy of the Hours is one of the richest prayer resources of the Christian Church, with prayers, psalms, and readings for each of the Hours, changing each day and through the seasons to keep us focused on God throughout the day and throughout the rhythm of seasons during the year. As we have discussed, with more than a thousand different Hours every year, the books used are many and thick and using them can be complex, so complex that it is rare to find anyone reciting the Hours apart from the clergy and highly religious.

Thankfully, there are now several resources available that make the Liturgy of the Hours more approachable for the average person. Also, to participate in the Liturgy of the Hours doesn't require participating in all seven prayer times. Myself, I like to participate in the morning, noon, and evening prayers as these fit most naturally into my daily life. Also, instead of the books, there are many phone apps that make the Liturgy of the Hours much more approachable.

Since the Liturgy of the Hours has historically been practiced in the Orthodox and Catholic faiths, this is where we will start.

Catholic Resources –

All Christians can benefit from the rich heritage found in the Catholic Liturgy of the Hours, although many Protestants may find a heavier emphasis on the Virgin Mary than they are comfortable with.

DivineOffice.org

A wonderful website with iOS and Android apps for the Liturgy of the Hours with wonderful audio recordings of all seven of the liturgies each day. This is by far my favorite app. Unfortunately, they are currently involved in a copyright dispute and have closed their ministry to new people while they go through the process of acquiring all permissions. They will still grant free access to priests, deacons, nuns, sisters, brothers and those who have been praying in the community, but failed to register. They will also grant access to anyone with disabilities.

Universalis.com

This has been a ministry dedicated to bringing the Liturgy of the Hours to everyone, everywhere. Their iOS and Android apps provide the complete daily office, all 7 offices, by providing the text and an audio recording so that you can follow by listening to the office. To hear the audio recording of the Liturgy of the Hours requires a monthly subscription, which is at a very reasonable cost.

Orthodox Resources –

There is a long, two millennium, tradition of fixed hour prayer within the Orthodox Church. Coming from the Protestant faith, I find the prayers often resonate with me more than those from the Catholic tradition, although many of the Bible translations used are older, along the lines of the King James Bible.

Pray Always app

There are both IOS and Android versions of this wonderful app that have the Liturgy of the Hours in the Orthodox tradition. The free app contains the Morning and Evening prayers as well as many other fixed prayers. The paid version also contains the midday prayer and many other fixed prayers.

Qleedo+

This app is available in IOS and Android versions that provide all 7 daily fixed hour prayers and comes from the Syrian Orthodox tradition. I have found this to be an easy app to use.

Non-Denominational Resources –

For those not of the Catholic, Orthodox, Anglican, or Episcopal faiths, they may find one of these more approachable.

Divine Hours

The Divine Hours provides a shortened office in a single volume for each season of the year and includes morning, mid-day, evening, and night time prayers. The Divine Hours is specifically suited to individual use and may be a good choice for those first wanting to approach fixed hour prayer. Beyond the books, Ann Arbor Vineyard Church provides the current Divine Hours prayer on their website: https://annarborvineyard.org/resources/pray-the-divine-hours/

Common Prayer: A Liturgy for Ordinary Radicals

Available in book form and with the daily readings at their website, commonprayer.net. On their website they describe the book, "*as a tapestry of daily prayers inviting faith communities from around the world to pray, sing, and act together. At this site, you'll find prayers for every evening, morning, and midday that celebrate the best of the Christian tradition and engage with the most pressing issues of our world today*". Each day, there is a new Morning Prayer. The Mid Day Prayer is the same each day and the Evening Prayers consist of 7 prayers, one for each day of the week, repeated each week. As they mention on their website, there is an emphasis on social causes, that some may or may not agree with. (Media, n.d.)

Once again, the principle is to not focus upon a single book, but to look at the principle of having set times of prayer, that focuses primarily on the attributes of God, throughout the day. There are many other resources available beyond those mentioned above, so I would focus on finding a book or app that works for you.

◆ ◆ ◆

Intercessory Prayer

God, you call us to care for one another. We pray: strengthen your servants, O God. (intercession, n.d.)

What does intercessory prayer mean in the context of our love of God? A follower of Jesus should strive to be Christ-like. One of the most important ways we can do this is in bearing each other's burdens, both physically and in prayer. Charles Williams coined a term "co-inherence". One of the ways in which he used that term is in the sense that we are all tied together, like the triune God, three in one, we as humans are all part of a greater whole. God calls us to care for one another. A prayer for a family member, a church member, a co-worker, a stranger, for someone we dislike, for a problem we can't understand. An intercession, feeling the pain of others. Taking some of the heaviness of life from friends, family, co-workers, and, as Jesus taught, even from those outside our comfort zone.

> *For all whose lives are stirred with faith and violence, despair and mistrust we pray: strengthen your servants, O Lord.*

As we try and see life from another's perspective, try to imagine what others are feeling, by seeing life from their point of view. A change begins in us and in the world around us. Thomas Merton often stated that he felt that it was the intercessory prayers of his fellow monks that was holding the world in balance. He felt that intercessory prayer was their work that was the most important of all. When we pray for others, when we put other's interests before our own, when we forgive, a weight is lifted, a veil is dropped, and we can see clearly that we are all one. All lovingly created. All in this life, gifted to us by God, together.

Praying for the homeless, for those in countries ravaged by war, for sick patients, for troubled class-mates, for strained family relationships. ... By praying for each other, by naming their worries, their concerns, we come that much closer to healing ourselves as well as those whose burdens we carry.

The daily examine, an Ignatian technique, of aligning ourselves and our actions with God's will is another opportunity for intercessory prayer. We will discuss this technique more fully later in the book, but by taking a few moments to pray in the morning and in the evening for others, we bookend our day with meaning. We plan and prepare in the morning and reflect and process in the evenings. Both times images of people come before us, people that need our prayer. We take on a portion of their burden in this way. We also think about ways in which we can help more, how we can order our lives for others.

For the homeless, for exiles, wanderers, and all who have no land to call home, we pray: strengthen your servants, O Lord.

This is the true meaning of Christianity. As Christ lived and died and rose again for us, as he turned the other cheek, walked the extra mile, gave his shirt when he was asked for just his coat, as he helped the sick, as he stood up for the weak and oppressed, as he instructed the confused and misled, as he put other's needs before his own, as he sent the Holy Spirit to live in us to guide and comfort us as we strive to seek the strength to do God's will in a difficult world, as Christ did all those things and more, we should do the same.

Let us intentionally pray for each other and perform acts of mercy, remembering that we all are broken and confused and oftentimes sleepwalking through life. We see Christ in the poor, the stranger, the enemy, the store clerk, the person who cuts us off in traffic, and those in need of our help. By training ourselves to notice the mystery of co-inherence and interdependence we, like the Trappist monks, will tighten the bonds of humanity.

For the sick, the troubled, the depressed, the aimless, and for those whose names and images come before our eyes this day we pray: strengthen your servants, O Lord.

◆ ◆ ◆

The Jesus Prayer

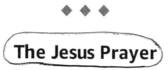

Common in the Eastern Orthodox tradition, the Jesus Prayer consists of a simple but powerful prayer "Lord Jesus Christ, Son of God, have mercy on me". Other variations of this include "Lord Jesus Christ, Son of God, have mercy on me, a sinner" or "Lord Jesus Christ, Son of God, have mercy on us."

As a means of ongoing contemplation throughout the day, it is recommended to say the Jesus Prayer out loud or silently throughout the day. Imagine reciting the prayer while standing in line to check out, while stuck in traffic, prior to going into a meeting, ... I particularly find it helpful when going in to see a patient to use the version, "Lord Jesus Christ, Son of God, have mercy on us." I use this in thinking about the challenges of human communication. Of the patient trying to communicate their problem to me, of my trying to understand, of me slowing down to listen, ... and of the challenges in interacting with someone who is in a different stage of life, who lives a different lifestyle, ...

Silently saying the prayer a hundred or more times a day, in a sense, imprints the prayer in your inner person. When stress or difficult situations arise, the practice is there beneath the surface and the prayer provides an underlying rhythm to help maintain an inner equilibrium.

The Four Strands (Ware K.)

I like this summary of the prayer by Kallistos Ware, an English Bishop in the Eastern Orthodox Church, which I will try and briefly paraphrase.

"Lord Jesus Christ, Son of God, have mercy on me." The Jesus Prayer is brief and concise - ten words in English, only seven in Greek or Russian - yet at the same time it is remarkably complete. Within this one short sentence we may find combined four 'strands' or constituent elements:

the cry for mercy;

the discipline of repetition;

the quest for stillness (hesychia1);

the veneration of the Holy Name.

So, what is the origin of these four elements, and how did they come together to form the Jesus Prayer?

1. The Cry for Mercy

"Lord, have mercy", Kyrie eleison, is found in liturgical worship from the 4th century, and its use in Christian prayer may well be more ancient. To ask for divine mercy is not to be seen as something exclusively penitential concerning our sin. While the cry for mercy certainly involves sorrow for sin, it speaks also of divine forgiveness. It affirms that God's loving kindness and compassion are greater than my brokenness and guilt. Mercy signifies precisely the love of God, poured out to heal and restore.

The Jesus Prayer, then, with its appeal for mercy, is not only a prayer of repentance, it is also a prayer full of light and hope. St Hesychius of Sinai (8th century) summed up its true spirit by saying, "If we unceasingly call upon Jesus with a keen yearning that is full of sweetness and joy, then the air of our heart is filled with rejoicing and peace. For me, in praying,

"Lord Jesus Christ, Son of God, have mercy on us." I find my focus is not only on God's mercy towards me, but that I also am invited to be God's light in a dark world by allowing Him to extend His mercy to others, through me. I am invited to extend mercy towards others, the same mercy that I am pleading for myself before God.

2. The Discipline of Repetition

This is first found in an explicit form among the Desert Fathers of Egypt in the 4th century. Their daily work was of a very simple kind, such as basket-making and the plaiting of rush mats. How was a monk to occupy his mind, as he undertook such uniform and monotonous tasks? How could he fulfil St Paul's injunction, "Pray without ceasing", 1 Th 5:17? One of the solutions adopted by the Desert Fathers was to practice 'monologic prayer', that is, the repetition of a single word or phrase. They found that this discipline of repetition helps to simplify the mind, bringing it from fragmentation to unity.

The phrases repeated by the ascetics of Egypt were often a verse from Scripture, and especially from the Psalms, such as Psalm 51:1, "Have mercy on me, O God, according to your steadfast love", or

Psalm 70:1, "Make haste, O God, to deliver me! O Lord, make haste to help me!" Non-Scriptural phrases could also be used. Abba Apollo sought to atone for a sin of his youth by repeating, "As man, I have sinned; as God, do You forgive." The Spiritual Homilies attributed to St Macarius in the late 4th century, include the prayer "I beseech You, I beseech You, O Lord." Other 'monologic prayers' used by Christians today, although not found among the Desert Fathers, include such phrases as "Lord, remember me in Your kingdom", and "Glory to You, O God, glory to You", an invocation occurring at the start of many Orthodox services.

3. The Quest for Stillness (Hesychia)

The third of our four strands also emerged among the monks of 4th-century Egypt. "When you pray," wrote Evagrius of Pontus (346-99), "do not shape within yourself any image of the Deity, and do not let your intellect be stamped with the impress of any form ... Prayer is a putting-away of thoughts." He did not, of course, intend this as a description of all forms of prayer, he was simply recommending, alongside liturgical worship and the study of Scripture, a particular type of prayer that may be called 'non-iconic', or what we are calling Centering Prayer. This same theme recurs in other Western texts, such as The Cloud of Unknowing in the 14th century and The Dark Night of the Soul by St John of the Cross in the 16th century.

Evagrius did not suggest any practical method for attaining 'non-iconic' prayer. In the 5th century, however, St Diadochus of Photike proposed the invocation of Jesus as precisely a way of entry into the prayer of inner stillness, "The intellect requires of us imperatively some task that will satisfy its need for activity. For the complete fulfilment of its purpose we should give it nothing but the prayer Lord Jesus... Let the intellect continually concentrate on these words within its inner shrine with such intensity that it is not turned aside to any mental images." In this way, Diadochus linked together two of the four strands, the discipline of repetition and the quest for hesychia. Repetition will assist us in stilling our ever-active mind, and so will enable us to acquire prayer of interior silence.

4. The Worship of the Holy Name

The Old Testament displays a profound reverence for the name of God, in the words of the prophet Malachi in Malachi 1:11, "From the rising of the sun to

its setting My name will be great among the nations."
So strong was the awe inspired by God's name that the
four consonants comprising the name 'YHWH', 'Lord'
- was not pronounced aloud in Judaism.

In the New Testament, the prayer to God the
Father that Christ shared with his disciples included
the phrase, "Hallowed be Thy name". At the Last Supper he went further, teaching them to pray not only in
the name of the Father but likewise in his own name,
John 16:23-24. Peter, in his confession of faith before
the Sanhedrin immediately after Pentecost, insisted
that there is no other name under heaven by which
we may be saved than Jesus Christ (Ac 4:10-12). "let it
be known to all of you and to all the people of Israel
that by the name of Jesus Christ of Nazareth, whom
you crucified, whom God raised from the dead—by
him this man is standing before you well. This Jesus
is the stone that was rejected by you, the builders,
which has become the cornerstone. And there is salvation in no one else, for there is no other name
under heaven given among men by which we must be
saved."

Indeed, the literal meaning of the name 'Jesus'
is precisely 'Savior'; as the angel said to Joseph, "You
shall call His name Jesus, for He will save His people

from their sins" (Mt 1:21). When we use the Jesus Prayer, we are thus reaffirming Jesus Christ as our personal Savior. In the same spirit, Paul regarded the name of Jesus as a focus of adoration: "At the name of Jesus every knee should bow" (Ph 2:10).

The early Church reaffirmed this devotion to the Divine Name. Hermas, the author of The Shepherd, in the second century stated, "The name of the Son of God is great and boundless, and it upholds the whole world." "Sufficient for our defense against our enemies is the name of Jesus Christ the most high God." wrote St Nilus of Ancyra in the fifth century. A similar love for the Holy Name was expressed in the medieval West, notably by St Bernard of Clairvaux (1090-1153). In the thirteenth century, paraphrasing Bernard, the Yorkshireman Richard Rolle, hermit of Hampole, exclaimed: "Ah! Ah! that wonderful name! Ah! that delectable name! This is the name that is above all names... Verily the name of Jesus is in my mind a joyous song, and heavenly music in mine ear, and in my mouth a honeyed sweetness."

So in summary, in the spirit of Lectio Divina, which we will discuss in the next chapter, consider reciting the Jesus Prayer aloud or silently, as you go through your day as a means of keeping God before you and a tool for working towards "Pray without ceasing".

Welcoming Prayer

So, I am going through my day. I've started the day with Centering Prayer, moved into the Liturgy of the Hours, had my coffee and left for work. I'm driving in my car, the radio is off, perhaps inwardly reciting the Jesus Prayer. Suddenly, a car runs a stop sign, I slam on my brakes to avoid hitting him, and I find myself overcome with rage! What to do? In another example, I'm happily working away in surgery, when suddenly things become difficult, a bleeding blood vessel that is hard to control, a large mass that highly distorts the anatomy making it hard to see a clear path forward. Fear begins to well up! What to do?

Although based on the 18th century classic *Abandonment to Divine Providence* by Jean-Pierre de Caussade, the Welcoming Prayer is not an ancient practice. Mary Mrozowski of Brooklyn, New York, one of the early leaders in the Centering Prayer movement, developed the method. Father Thomas Keating and others saw the value of her little method and over the years it has been supported, fine-tuned and expanded within the community of people who practice centering prayer and beyond. The Welcoming Prayer also involves consent, abandonment, surrender, and trust of the transformative presence of God. It acknowledges the reality of current circumstances and invites the awareness of the divine within that space. The Welcoming Prayer is designed to complement Centering Prayer which teaches us consenting in stillness. The Welcoming Prayer teaches us consenting in activity.

> *Like Martha and Mary, Centering Prayer and the Welcoming Prayer complement one another with balance and wholeness. With that balance and wholeness, what was once separate experiences become one seamless experience. With the Welcoming Prayer, prayer becomes alive in action. This prayer can be especially helpful throughout the day as we find times of stress and thoughts and feelings contrary to God arise. I like this quote from the Contemplative Life series from Contemplative Outreach:*

> *Martha and Mary are two complementary dimensions of our humanness. Without Mary's*

stillness at the center -sitting at the feet of the Teacher and listening - we become like Martha, worried and discontented. There is nothing wrong with Martha's activity. It is her motivation or intention that is in question. Her anxiety and worry keep her in turmoil and prevent her from being present. She is troubled about many things but only one is necessary. The roar of the Martha mind and emotions drown out the Mary heart. Before we know it we are acting as if we are separate from God or God is absent.

This story is a wonderful example of the focus we can bring to everyday life activities. Mary and Martha are like two lenses; through the process of transformation these two ways of seeing and being can become one. We usually live alternating between the two lenses, now active, now contemplative, back and forth. Through our practices and God's grace, these two lenses may come into alignment so that we are able to rest in God in all activity, becoming true contemplatives in action.

What then is the Welcoming Prayer? When circumstances arise and you find yourself turning from

God, struggling with a particular feeling or emotion, particularly a bad one, such as rage towards the driver who ran the stop sign, this method offers a structured way to embrace and accept it, so you can release it and move on. In this practice there are three phases to the Prayer. You might go directly from one to the next in a single, relatively formulaic prayer sequence or you might find yourself staying in one phase for some time as it does its interior work in you. Using Cynthia Bourgeault's labels, the three parts are:

Focus and sink in.

Welcome.

Let go.

Focus and Sink In

This is not about indulging bad feelings. It's not about amplifying them or justifying them. It's about feeling the feeling. Allow yourself to become immersed in it. Let it wash over you, don't run away from it or fight it. Just feel what it's like to be experiencing it.

The word "feel" can mean either to have a physical experience of touching, or to have a mental experience of encountering an emotion. Connect those two. Feel the emotion physically. Notice your body, the changes that come over your body as you are tense, anxious, or angry. As with meditation, you are just observing the feeling, not trying to alter it.

Welcome

You can only start from where you are, and you can only move forward if you accept where you are. Affirm the rightness of where you are by welcoming the bad feeling or emotion and acknowledging God's presence in the moment. You do this by literally saying, "Welcome, [bad feeling]." If you are frozen in fear, say, "Welcome, fear." Hot with rage: say, "Welcome, rage." Note we're talking here about feelings and emotions, not problems and physical hardships. We are not welcoming illness or injustice. The welcoming prayer is for feelings and emotions, not what triggered them.

Many resist the idea of accepting where they are at, of accepting the emotion when the emotion is not good and appears contrary to God. There is nothing passive though about acceptance. Acceptance merely establishes you in reality, so that you can respond to the situation and the emotion effectively.

David DeShan M.D.

If you are terrified about a health issue, that fear may be immobilizing you; accepting the fear and then releasing the fear may free you to be able to deal with the issue.

Let Go

There are at least four ways to let go in the welcoming prayer. Mary Mrozowski's original version uses a fixed statement. You say these lines no matter what the specific issue:

Welcome, welcome, welcome.

I welcome everything that comes to me in this moment because I know it is for my healing.

I welcome all thoughts, feelings, emotions, persons, situations and conditions.

I let go of my desire for security. I let go of my desire for approval.

I let go of my desire for control.

I let go of my desire to change any situation, condition, person, or myself.

I open to the love and presence of God and the healing action and grace within.

Personally, I am a quick start and I find the entire pray above rather long and cumbersome. My favorite version of the prayer is, "I let go of my desire for security, affection, and control. I let go of the desire to change what I am experiencing."

God is with us and loves us personally and uniquely, without exception. The Welcoming Prayer encourages an acknowledgement of our feelings and emotions, which are often beyond our control. It recognizes that nothing comes to us apart from God. It allows a returning to a relationship with the Spirit of God within us and an opportunity for recognizing the presence and action of the Spirit in our lives now, despite the circumstance or our feelings.

The Guest House

·

This being human is a guest house
Every morning a new arrival.

A joy, a depression, a meanness,
Some momentary awareness comes
As an unexpected visitor.

Welcome and entertain them all
Even if they're a crowd of sorrows,
Who violently sweep your house
empty of its furniture.

Still, treat each guest honorably,
He may be cleaning you out for
some new delight.

The dark thought, the shame, the malice,
Meet them at door laughing and invite them in.
Be grateful for whoever comes,
Because each has been sent
As a guide from beyond.

~Rumi

MEDITATE ON SCRIPTURE

The gratuity of Lectio Divina is different from the utility of study. Study endeavors to master the Word. Lectio Divina surrenders and yields before the Word.

~ Father Bernardo Olivera

Lectio Divina

Lectio Divina or divine reading, is one of the great treasures of the Christian tradition of prayer. The founders of the medieval tradition of Lectio Divina were Saint Benedict and Pope Gregory I and it became a regular practice in Benedictine monasteries by the 6th century. However, the methods that they employed had precedents dating back to Origen in the third century and back to biblical times in the Hebrew. Lectio Divina is a way of reading Scriptures consisting of multiple slow readings of a small section of Scripture. Instead of analyzing the passage only for knowledge, we open ourselves to the words, we rest in the words, we partake of the words, opening our inmost being to the possibility of insight and transformation at a much deeper level. The idea is to listens to the text of the Bible with the "ear of the heart".

This tradition of prayer flows out of a Hebrew method of reading the Haggadah, a text read during Passover that retells the Exodus story. Haggadah means "telling" and is an interpretation for telling and retelling the story of Passover. It was part of the devotional practice of the Jews in the days of Jesus.

Listening to the word of God in Scripture by Lectio Divina is a traditional way of cultivating friendship with God. It is a way of listening to the texts of Scripture as if we are in conversation with God. This daily encounter with and reflection on His word leads beyond mere acquaintanceship to an attitude of friendship, trust, and love. Conversation simplifies and gives way to communing. Gregory the Great, from the sixth century, in summarizing the Christian contemplative tradition expressed it as "resting in God." This was the classical meaning of Contemplative Prayer in the Christian tradition for the first sixteen centuries.

The classical practice of Lectio Divina can be divided into two forms: monastic and scholastic. The scholastic form is more formalized and was developed in the twelfth century. This method divides the process of Lectio Divina into four hierarchical, consecutive steps: reading, reflecting, responding and resting.

The first stage is *Lectio* or reading. We read the word slowly and reflectively, steeping ourselves in it. Short sections, a couple of verses at a time, work best for this practice. There are also many other sources for short daily meditations, whether in the Book of Common Prayer, the Philokalia, or other devotional sources, often associated with monastic or contemplative orders.

The second stage is *Meditatio* or reflection. We simply reflect deeply on the words and images of the text.

The third stage is *Oratio* or response. We leave our thinking aside and simply let our hearts speak to God. This response is inspired by our reflection on the Word of God or the other devotional reading we have chosen.

The fourth stage of Lectio Divina is *Contemplatio* or rest. As much as possible, we let go of all thought and simply rest in the word, listening at the deepest level of our being. We open ourselves to an inner transformation and realignment according to the divine presence.

The monastic form of Lectio Divina is a more ancient method in which reading, reflecting, responding and resting are experienced as moments rather than steps in a process. In this form, the interaction among the moments is dynamic and the movement through the moments follows the spontaneous prompting of the Holy Spirit. To allow for this spontaneity, this method of Lectio Divina is practiced in private. In the monastic form, one reads or listens to the word of God in a particular passage chosen for the occasion and then the only process is to follow the attraction of the Spirit.

For example:

> Read the passage slowly, after a minute or two of silence, read it again. As you listen you may be aware of a phrase, sentence, insight or even a word in the sense of "message" that catches your attention (reading).

> Sit with that phrase, sentence, insight or word, repeating it gently over and over in your heart, not thinking about it but just being with it. (pondering it in your heart).

> Be aware of any prayer that rises up within you that expresses what you are experiencing (responding).

> Or just rest in the phrase, sentence, insight or even one word, resting in God beyond your thoughts, reflections, and particular prayer. Resting in God in the simple attraction of inter-

ior silence (resting).

These are general guidelines, not a fixed, formal sequence. The natural movement of the practice is toward an inner silence, allowing deep to call out to deep.

The practice can be done individually or as a group, but if as a group, the scholastic form is usually followed and a facilitator would be required to indicate the movement to the next stage. There will be less fluid back and forth between the stages than with an individual practice.

Once again, you are invited to savor

this 'secret chain' of texts

given to the pilgrim

as a scriptural 'map'

of how prayer may move deeply into the heart.

~excerpted and edited from The Pilgrim Continues His Way

So I want you to understand clearly

that for beginners and those a little advanced

in contemplation,

reading or hearing the Word of God

must precede pondering it and

without time given to serious reflection

there will be no genuine prayer.

~Cloud of Unknowing, chapter 35

Gospel Meditation

When asked about his spiritual exercises to come to know Christ, so that one may love him in a more real way, Saint Ignatius Loyola, a 16th-century Spanish priest, theologian, and founder of the Society of Jesus (Jesuits), invited people to engage in a prayer method he called, "application of the senses". In this method you use your senses in an imaginative way to reflect on a Gospel passage. You use your senses of, seeing, hearing, tasting, touching, and smelling to make the Gospel scene real and alive.

Here is a way of engaging in this prayer form which is relaxing and rather easy.

Select a passage from one of the Gospels in which Jesus is interacting with others.

Read the Gospel passage twice so that the story and the details of the story become familiar.

Close your eyes and reconstruct the scene in your imagination. See what is going on and watch the men and women in the scene. What does Jesus look like? How do the others react to him? What are the people saying to one another? What emotions fill their words? Is Jesus touching someone? As you enter into the scene, there can be the desire to be there. Place yourself in the scene, perhaps as an observer, as one lining up for healing, or as one helping others to Jesus.

Some people's imaginations are very active, so they construct a movie-like scenario with a Gospel passage. Others will enter the scene with verbal imagination, reflecting on the scene and mulling over the actions. Vividness is not a criterion for the effectiveness of this kind of prayer. Engagement in the story results in a more interior knowledge of Jesus.

As you finish this time of prayer, you should take a moment to speak person to person with Christ saying what comes from the heart. (Praying with Scripture,

Memorizing Scripture

Jesus says, "If you abide in me, and my words abide in you, ask whatever you wish, and it will be done for you." Having God's Word abiding within us begins with memorization. What can I say about memorizing scripture that has not been said before.

Dallas Willard, professor of Philosophy at the University of Southern California, wrote, "Bible memorization is absolutely fundamental to spiritual formation. If I had to choose between all the disciplines of the spiritual life, I would choose Bible memorization, because it is a fundamental way of filling our minds with what it needs. This book of the law shall not depart out of your mouth. That's where you need it! How does it get in your mouth? Memorization" (Willard, Spring 2001)

Chuck Swindoll wrote, "I know of no other single practice in the Christian life more rewarding, practically speaking, than memorizing Scripture. . .. No other single exercise pays greater spiritual dividends! Your prayer life will be strengthened. Your witnessing will be sharper and much more effective. Your attitudes and outlook will begin to change. Your mind will become alert and observant. Your confidence and assurance will be enhanced. Your faith will be solidified". (Swindoll)

Abiding in God and abiding in His word, is our goal. Abiding begins with memorization, but doesn't end there. As both Dallas Willard and Chuck Swindoll implied, memorization is the start to abiding in His word. Coupling memorization with Lectio Divina truly allows God's Word to begin abiding within us, and allows Him to use the power of His word in our spiritual transformation.

PRACTICE HUMILITY

Simplicity is forgetfulness of self and remembrance of our humble status as waiting servants of God.

~ Quaker Doctrine

The Sin of Pride

The sin of pride is considered by many to be the sin of sins. It was pride which transformed Lucifer, an anointed cherub of God, the very "seal of perfection, full of wisdom and perfect in beauty", (Ez. 28:12) into Satan, the devil, the father of lies, the one for whom Hell itself was created. (Jn. 8:44)   It was the sin of pride which first led Eve to eat of the forbidden fruit.

St. Augustine of Hippo, quoting from Ecclesiastes, wrote, "'Pride is the commencement of all sin' because it was this which overthrew the devil, from whom arose the origin of sin; and afterwards, when his malice and envy pursued man, who was yet standing in his uprightness, it subverted him in the same way in which he himself fell. For the serpent, in fact, only sought for the door of pride whereby to enter when he said, 'Ye shall be as gods.'" (Schaff)

In summarizing the sin of pride and man lifting himself up like God, I think no one better summarizes pride better than Friedrich Nietzsche, "If we could communicate with the gnat, we would learn that he likewise flies through the air with the same solemnity, that he feels the flying center of the universe within himself." (Nietzsche)

How do we overcome pride? In short, we can't, it is only the work of God within us that can overcome pride. The moment we say on our own, "I have overcome pride", we are taking pride in our own humility! This becomes an endless circular trap! What are we to do? There is much wisdom to be gained by learning from those who have gone before, who developed practices of daily living that help us align our heart with God, which allows God to work within our heart. We will look at four such practices in this chapter.

❖ ❖ ❖

The Rule of St. Benedict and the Twelve Steps of Humility

In chapter 7 of his Rule for life in a monastic community, St Benedict describes twelve steps of humility, which each monk is to consider and undertake if he is ever to increase in love as an adopted son of God. St. Benedict begins by noting, "Whoever exalts himself shall be humbled, and whoever humbles himself shall be exalted", as a summation of Luke 14:11 and 18:14. He then goes on to say that those who want to reach the highest summit of humility must shun pride and exaltation, and just as well that our actions will be like a ladder to heaven which Jacob saw in his dream in Genesis 28 where the angels ascended and descended. St. Benedict writes that to ascend the ladder of humility to Heaven one must lower himself and to descend the ladder away from Heaven one would have to exalt himself.

Briefly, his twelve steps are:

1. The Fear of God - That a man keeps the fear of God always before his eyes (Psalm 36:2)

2. Not my will, but Yours O Lord - A man loves not his own will nor takes pleasure in the satisfaction of his desires; rather he shall imitate by his actions that saying of the Lord: For I have come down from heaven, not to do my own will, but the will of Him who sent me." (John 6:38)

3. Obedience to our superiors – He was obedient even unto death (Philippians 2:8). In this step we must submit ourselves to the yoke of Christ which He Himself bore in humility and obedience, even obedience unto death, death on a cross. And so then we must submit ourselves to God's care, especially to the care of those who are our superiors.

4. Embrace suffering patiently and obediently - Obedience under difficult, unfavorable, or even unjust conditions, "his heart quietly embraces suffering and endures it without weakening or seeking escape." To which St. Benedict adds from Scripture, but the one who endures to the end will be saved (Matt 10:22) and to which we might add "Then Jesus told his disciples: If anyone would come after me, let him deny himself and take up his cross and follow me. For whoever would save his life, will lose it: but whoever loses his life for my sake will find it." (Matthew 16:24-25)

5. Confess your sins and faults - Regularly confess one's sins, and in St. Benedict's rule it is clear that he writes that monks confess directly to their abbot any sinful thoughts that they have in their hearts or any secret wrongdoings that they have committed against him or others. Of course, you may not have an abbot, but having a friend, spouse, pastor, who is on a similar journey, to confide in and confess to can fill this void.

6. Content yourself with lowliness - Content ourselves with lowliness and to accept the lowest ranks and treatment that others have to offer. We recognize our sinfulness and our frailty and in such a manner recognize that of our own selves, left to our own devices, we are of little value, and yet not of no value because God saw in us a precious value so as to atone for our sins and bring us into His life. We are of little value because of our sins but of great value on account of the image we behold of Him. Thus we must sing with the Psalmist, "I was brutish and ignorant; I was like a beast towards you. Nevertheless, I am continually with you; you hold my right hand." (Psalm 73:22-23)

7. Interior mediocrity - Recognize and admit not only with our voice but with the fullness of our heart that we are inferior to all because of how we have been given specific, unique, and beloved gifts of God which we have squandered. They were specific to us and beautifully made for us specifically, but we spoiled God's gifts and abused them. For this, we ought to consider ourselves inferior to others on account of how we abused ourselves through our sins and how we abused God's gifts.

8. To keep the rule - A Benedictine monk to uphold the common rule of the monastery and to follow the example of his superiors.

9. Silence and solitude – A monk ought only speak when questioned by his superiors or by others, and in all other matters hold his tongue. Do we avoid speaking ill of others, or embrace silence and solitude whenever God provides for us? Do we avoid listening to too much music or watching to many videos, sports games, playing to many video games, ... so as to keep our internal tongue (our mind's tongue) silent and awaiting the contemplation of God in every moment? Remain silent in the heart and in the tongue, for God's first language, St. John of the Cross says, is silence. So too then embrace a calm and peaceful desire for solitude, only seeking to speak when spoken too, or of pressing manners, not wasting our tongue on things that do not need to be said or saying things that ought not be said.

10 Keep your peace in times of laughter - Avoid excessive laughter. This may sound excessive, but there is a certain extent to which joking around too much, or acting a fool can be a major distraction and even arise to use making fun of holy things. Laughing at people or things which are not humorous or good-natured is to show a sort of superiority over a thing, to point to the silliness of a thing and to place yourself above it. So then for the lay person we must be careful not to laugh at things such as people falling down, or to put people down as we perceive their failures. One is entitled to joy and laughter, but not a condescending laughter which ruins humility and meekness.

11. Speak calmly and modestly - As the tongue is difficult to control and lends us over to quick decisions, so we must train the heart and the tongue to speak modestly, without laughter, gently, lovingly, endearingly, and forever to be conscious of our divine destination. A wise man is known by his few words.

12. Everlasting humility and meekness - The final step of humility is to bear all these things in one's heart at all manners of the night and day. In this manner the work of God will be manifest to others and though the monk prays and fasts secretly in his closet and not publicly, his deeds and holiness will shine forth. His contrition for his sins will forever be on his mind, though he will be mindful of the great gifts God has given him, taking care not to squander them. No matter what ordinary or small deed the humble man does it will all be done with the greatest care and offering up to the Lord. In this manner then, perfect love is bloomed.

Ignatius Examen

This practice is a staple of Ignatian spirituality, as practiced by St. Ignatius, founder of the Society of Jesus or Jesuit order. The Jesuit practice is to see God in all things. The Examen is a reflective practice to be done every day that brings awareness of God at work in our life throughout the day. The Examen is not primarily concerned with our good and bad actions, but rather with our thoughts and impulses that underlie them and in becoming sensitive to and seeing God presence throughout the day.

1. To begin, sit quietly at the end of the day and ask to see your day through the light of God's eyes

2. Give thanks for the gift of this day.

3. Carefully look back at your experiences of the day, reflecting on where God was present in events, people, and experiences.

4. Be sensitive to shortcomings in life or areas that need attention. Hold them in your awareness and be present with them.

5. Ask for wisdom to discern God's presence in the day to come.

◆ ◆ ◆

Simplicity

"...our chief, in fact our only task, is to get rid of the 'double' garment, the overlaying layer of duplicity that is not ourselves." ~Thomas Merton on finding our true self.

If the first step in the Cistercian ascent to God is for the monk to *know himself* we may reasonably say that, in some sense, the whole of such a one's life will consist in *being himself*, or rather trying to return to the original simplicity, immortality and freedom which constitute his real self, in the image of God. (St Bernard, Thomas Merton & Simplicity, n.d.)

We will never completely succeed in being ourselves until we get to heaven. Meanwhile on earth our chief, in fact our only task, is to get rid of the 'double' garment, the overlaying layer of duplicity that is not ourselves. Hence the Cistercian stress on simplicity, in fact the whole of Cistercian asceticism may be summed up in that one word. This is true even when the word is taken in several different senses.

The first step in the monks' ascent to God will be to recognize the truth about himself–and face the fact of his own duplicity. That means *simplicity in the sense of sincerity,* a frank awareness of one's own shortcomings.

In the second step, he will also have to overcome the temptation to excuse himself and argue that this is not, in fact, what he is. Whether he argues with other men, with himself or with God, it does not matter. Hence: *simplicity in the sense of meekness,* self-effacement, humility.

In the third step, he must strive to rid himself of everything that is useless, unnecessary to his one big end: the recovery of the divine image, and union with God. Simplicity takes on the sense of total and uncompromising *mortification:*

> **Of the lower appetites:** hence the simplicity in food, clothing, dwellings, labor, manner of life as laid down in the Little Exordium, Consuetudines, Statutes of the General Chapters [CS-these are Trappist and Cistercian monastic organizational documents].

> **Of the interior senses and the intellect:** This means simplicity in devotions, studies, methods of prayer, etc., and calls for the complete simplification in liturgical matters and

the decoration of churches for which the early Cistercians were so famous.

Of the will: This is the most important task of all. In the works of St. Bernard, the amount of space devoted to other forms of mortification is practically insignificant in comparison to the scores of pages which are given to the attachment on self-will and its utter destruction. Hence the stress on this means of penance, which is above all others for the monk: obedience. This will produce that simplicity, which is synonymous with docility, the trustful obedience of a child towards his father; the supernatural, joyous obedience of the monk who seeks to prove his love for Christ by seeing him in his representative, the abbot, or for us our church leadership.

Deep Listening

Deep Listening is respecting others and placing them above yourself. It is not time efficient. Good listening requires an inner self-discipline that keeps distracting thoughts and emotions from impeding the listening process. If you are really listening, you can't be always thinking about what you'll say next. That's hard, and it requires deep restraint. If you're listening for God, you need to focus on listening, not on preparing your response. This kind of self-control is difficult to achieve and requires a level of commitment and concentration that is hard to find in our busy, active cultures.

Listening also requires a posture of humility. If you're really going to hear God and others, you have to be open to not being right and to seeing something new. Several inner convictions and attitudes make humility in listening more difficult to achieve, including thinking we already know answers and loving action and activity.

Humility is necessary in order to listen when we suspect we already know what the other person will say. Humility is necessary to lay aside battle positions with someone we know we disagree with. Humility is necessary to set aside what we think we know based on our own prejudiced media accounts. Humility is necessary to listen to those outside the church in order to listen to their specific beliefs, priorities and feelings. Humility is necessary to slow down our activities long enough to pay attention to the words and feelings of the people around us.

Deep listening is a process of listening to learn. It requires the temporary suspension of judgment, and a willingness to receive new information, whether pleasant, unpleasant, or neutral.

Deep Listening Happens at Several Levels (Deep listening, n.d.)

> The **intrapersonal** level, at which an individual is listening deeply to his or her own interior experience. Think of practicing silence as deep listening to God.

> The **interpersonal** level, at which one individual is focused on listening to one or more others. We are often preoccupied by thinking about what we will say when it is our turn to speak. But it is how we listen that is transformative, especially in groups.

> The **group** level, at which one or more individuals is listening deeply to the voices of many others.

The Role of Questions

Questions are an integral part of deep listening.

Formulating a question takes thoughtfulness and implies that you are truly listening. Powerful questions also tend to draw you deeper into the conversation and inspire curiosity and learning. Powerful questions also put our focus on the meaning and possibilities of what the other is saying and creates an ongoing opportunity for introspection and reflection.

Principles for Deep Listening

To summarize the power of deep listening. How should we approach a conversation with deep listening in mind? Listen to learn, listen for understanding rather than agreement, and ask powerful questions.

FORM AUTHENTIC COMMUNITY

The love we give each other
Is that which builds us up.
We live in one another;
We share a common cup. ...
~ Haskell Miller

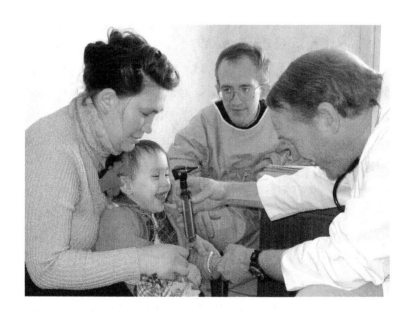

Importance of Community

The importance of community life is another great theme of Benedict's Rule. Prior to Benedict, religious life was the life of the hermit, who went to the desert and lived alone in order to seek God. Benedict's genius was understanding that each person's rough edges, all the defenses and pretensions and blind spots that keep the monastic from growing spiritually, are best confronted by living side by side with other flawed human beings whose faults and failings are only too obvious. St. Benedict teaches that growth comes from accepting people as they are, not as we would like them to be. His references to the stubborn and the dull, the undisciplined and the restless, the careless and the scatterbrained have the ring of reality. Though Benedict was no idealist with respect to human nature, he understood that the key to spiritual progress lies in constantly making the effort to see Christ in each person, no matter how irritating or tiresome. This then stresses the importance of living out our Christian faith in community, in the community of believers that is our local church and in the greater community that God has placed us into. Looking at living life in community, there are several particular aspects that I would like to explore.

Practice Hospitality

One of the highest values of Benedictine life is hospitality. Benedict of Nursia in his Rule of Life for monks and nuns wrote, "Let all guests who arrive be received like Christ." Receive every person who comes through your door as though they were bringing Jesus to you. Receive every person you meet as though you were encountering the face of Christ. (Meeting Jesus Through Hospitality, n.d.)

Intimacy with God results in intimacy with humanity. The oneness with all creation is real and palpable. A disposition of hospitality reflects a new understanding and experience of this oneness; our open, loving service to others is a form of stewardship for all of God's creation and is the way we honor and celebrate what we experience interiorly.

Part of what makes a monastery a healthy place is the receiving of guests, so that the monks or sisters don't get turned in on themselves, or imagine that they are the center of the world, or that only they are good Christians. This can also be applied to churches. What can help make them healthy is to receive guests, so that as members of the church, we don't imagine we're a club, or a secret society.

A church should be a place anyone can come to meet Jesus, and a church is a place where anyone who comes can be a way for the others there to meet Jesus. Of course, what is true of monasteries and churches is also true of us as individuals. Hospitality should be a central aspect of our lives in community.

◆ ◆ ◆

Practice Your Vocation As Unto the Lord

*"Lord of all pots and pans and things
make me a saint by getting meals and
washing up the plates!"*

~ Brother Lawrence

Brother Lawrence was a humble and godly monk who lived in France during the seventeenth century. He was an ex-soldier who was wounded in Thirty Years War. After being wounded, he returned home to his parent's house and while recovering he decided to pursue a more holy profession. (God is Amongst the Pots and Pans, n.d.)

After he became a monk, he discovered a priceless secret of the Christian life: how to practice the presence of God. He wrote that "all we have to do is to recognize God as being intimately within us." He served as a humble cook in the monastery kitchen. In the kitchen, he learned an important lesson through each of his daily chores: the time spent in prayer should be the same as the time spent doing chores. He believed "it was a serious mistake to think of our prayer time as being different from any other. Our actions should unite us with God when we are involved in our daily activities, just as our prayers unite us with him in our quiet devotions." He also wrote, "It isn't necessary that we stay in church in order to remain in God's presence. We can make our hearts personal chapels where we can enter anytime to talk to God privately."

What better way to serve in our community than to look at our work as prayer, done "unto the Lord". I am a physician and have often heard that I have a wonderful profession as I get to serve and care for people throughout the day. This is true, but it is also true of all professions. Yes, people see my work as in the service of others, but I also truly appreciate others who serve me cheerfully and take pride in their work. There is no job that this doesn't apply to, from garbage collector, to housekeeper, to construction worker, to fast food provider, to accountant, to lawyer, to stewardess, to pilot, to employer, ...

In this way, whatever we do, becomes a time of prayer, united with God, in service to one another, our community.

Be Involved in Your Local Church

Paul first reminds the Corinthian Christians, and us today, that as members of the body of Christ they constitute one body. The body is a natural symbol and a powerful image. Consider your own body, how all its parts must work together and how no part can be hurt without the whole body being hurt. In antiquity, as today, the image of body was often applied to cities and other social entities. But the body of Christ is not just another social organization, or another coalition of like-minded persons united in a voluntary association. It is the body of Christ. Christ makes this body different, Christ comes first, Christ unites the body. Our vertical relationship with Christ has as its necessary consequence our horizontal relationship with one another. As a member of the church, if you don't play your role within the body, then the whole body suffers.

In 1 Corinthians 10, Paul relates the body of Christ that we constitute as Christians with the body of Christ that we share in Communion. Sharing in Communion has always been a central part of monastic life as sharing the one bread and the one cup is a powerful sign of our oneness in Christ. By participating in the Communion meal, we express our unity with Christ and with one another. Thus, Communion is profoundly social, as is anytime we sit with others and share a meal together.

Behold Others and Nature

"Wisdom does not inspect but behold. We must look a long time before we can see."
~ Henry David Thoreau

What I mean by this is to focus with a long gaze of 15 seconds or more on another person or something beautiful around us. Isn't this what we do when gazing into the eyes of our lover, our children, when observing a beautiful painting, or scenic overlook?

Beholding changes the ways in which we see the world, enhancing one of the primary means through which we interact with the world: sight.

Joanna Ziegler, professor of Visual Arts and Art History at Holy Cross, was a pioneer of the contemplative practice of beholding and its application in the classroom. Ziegler found a way to deepen her connection to her discipline by developing methods that make use of studio habits like persistence and attentive observation.

She would have her students look at one abstract painting for an entire semester. Just one painting. Every week, they would visit the Worcester Art Museum, going to the museum at the same time, on the same day of the week, using the same mode of transportation, to sit in front of that one painting and respond to the question: What do you see?

They were instructed to refrain from research, consulting secondary sources, Googling, reading the wall text, or even speaking to docents, so that they could hear their own voices. Ziegler also asked them to report on subjective features of themselves as observers: how they felt physically and emotionally, and what was going on in their lives. She left the theoretical art history until the end of the course, when students were better able to take it in without affecting their experience of their painting. During their discussions of their experience up to that point, they learned to share their perceptions and ask the questions, what did we see, and do we have to agree on what we see before we interpret it?

Ziegler understood that through attending to and developing a feeling for great works of art, her students would become more interested in, develop an intimacy with the art, and begin to love what they had come to know. Repetition is a strong feature of her method. As her students went at the same time, to the same place each day, to sit before the same painting, and simply look, focusing their attention again and again, they noticed the changes they saw in the painting, and they also noticed changes in themselves. (Beholding)

On a similar note, I am not sure if this is true, but I have heard it described this way and it seems to be true in my life. See what you think:

Neuroscience can prove that whenever something negative, fearful, or critical comes our way, it attaches to our minds like Velcro. We know this to be true.

If we go through our day and have twenty-five positive encounters and one negative, which one keeps us awake all night ruminating? Fretting? Coming unglued? The one negative. Velcro.

And the opposite, according to neuroscientists is also true:

Anything hopeful, joyous, hits the mind like Teflon. In other words, those positive, encouraging thoughts come and go almost immediately, while the negative, fearful thoughts attach and stay.

Therefore, in order for the joyous, encouraging thoughts and experiences to attach and stay, to imprint on our brains, we must savor the positive moment for at least 15 seconds. Enjoy completely for 15 seconds. Less than 15 seconds, it doesn't imprint on the brain. (15 seconds to joy, n.d.)

How has this played out in my life? I try and pause more, look longer at a sunset, listen longer to a song bird, watch children playing in a park. In doing so, an amazing thing happens. I find it is difficult to fill my mind with negative thoughts and feelings when gazing upon beauty or the innocence of children.

How does this play out in church and community? Through the last 38 years at my local church, I have found that preachers have come and gone, worship has changed for the better or worse, people have come and gone. I can find myself dwelling on what was, what I used to like better, what I don't like about the music or the sermon, ... For me, beholding is the best way to combat this. If I find my mind wandering or turning negative during worship, communion, the sermon, ... I fix my gaze upon someone on the worship team, the pastor, or others in the congregation across the auditorium and just behold them for 15 seconds. During this time, I pray for the struggles in their life, for how they have impacted my life, for the gift they provide in our community, for the Joy God receives in beholding them. What happens? I can't harbor negative thoughts when focusing on the positive and trying to look at people and events through God's eyes. Over time, when I encounter these people again, my mind tends to return to the positive, recalling the thoughts and prayers I had while beholding them before.

Volunteer in Your Community, Particularly in Serving the Poor

An armor-clad knight with a lance, oil-tempered sword and plumed helmet rode his war charger out of Assisi to battle against his neighboring Italian town of Perugia. When this brave youth, Francesco Bernardone, saw the wretched specter of a leper in the road, he spurred his horse to flee. As he galloped by, Francis thought he recognized Christ in the contorted face of the outcast. Abruptly he stopped, dismounted, kissed the leper, gave him alms, seated the man on his horse, and led the way to the leper's destination.

Before this experience, Francis so loathed the sight of lepers that he would look at their houses only from a distance of two miles while holding his nose. Francis later said of this experience, "What had previously nauseated me became a source of spiritual and physical consolation.... After that I did not wait long before leaving the world."

For Francis, leaving the world meant turning away from his prior life, caring for lepers, and praying in deserted chapels.

In all monastic orders, but particularly the friars

and poor Clare's who follow St Francis, they are called to live in dependence on God through identifying with people around them who are poor, living a simple lifestyle and sharing all things in common. Their poverty extends beyond material poverty to an "attitude of the heart". Embracing this attitude, they strive to identify with the needs of the poor in our world and share their gifts, talents, ideas, resources and prayer life with them. (St Francis of Asisi On Joy of Poverty and Value of Dung, n.d.)

Find Like-Minded People for Mutual Encouragement Along the Path

In talking with others on a similar journey, seeking a deeper contemplative life, an oft heard phrase is similar to this one, which I recently heard, *"For many years there has been a deep longing in me to know God in a deeper, vital, experiential way. My church tradition is, I believe, somewhat similar to yours and it has been dominated by a focus on doctrine and the teaching of Scripture. My reading of Nouwen, Brother Lawrence and others over the years really drew me in, but it has been mostly solo journey with not too many with whom I could be too open about the deeper longings."*

One consequence of this desire for something more and this feeling of isolation can be a lashing out at the church, your spiritual community, and the focus on doctrine that got you to the very point of wanting more in a deeper contemplative relationship with God. This is where finding others along a similar path, even if in other denominations, and a spiritual guide can be exceptionally helpful. The solution for a deeper contemplative path is not found in lashing out at what brought you to the path of wanting more. God never intended for us to do life in isolation; we were made for community and fellowship with God and with one another.

If you can't find a local community, then an online community can be helpful. I have listed several possible communities in the Diving Deeper section. Of course, a local community is preferred as an online community cannot fully replace the personal interaction that comes meeting face to face.

ICON OF THE HOLY TRINITY

And the LORD appeared to Abraham by the oaks of Mamre, as he sat at the door of his tent in the heat of the day. He lifted up his eyes and looked, and behold, three men stood in front of him. When he saw them, he ran from the tent door to meet them, and bowed himself to the earth, and said, "My lord, if I have found favor in your sight, do not pass by your servant. Let a little water be brought, and wash your feet, and rest yourselves under the tree, while I fetch a morsel of bread, that you may refresh yourselves, and after that you may pass on - since you have come to your servant." So they said, "Do as you have said." (Gen 18:1-5)

With my exploration of Orthodoxy, came a need and a desire to better understand the role of icons in the Orthodox church. As I explored icons, the meaning of them and the rules that govern this form of worship, I encountered two icons that truly resonate with my soul. In this chapter, I will limit the discussion to just one, The Icon of the Holy Trinity. I hope you come away with some appreciation of the power and beauty of icons through this examination of the

Icon of the Holy Trinity.

One difference between my Protestant roots and Orthodoxy is that Protestants tend to start with the "One God" and divide it into the three of the Trinity, Father, Son, and Holy Spirit. The Orthodox tend to start with the three, the Father, the Son, and the Holy Spirit and through the relationship of the three, a tight bond is formed that unites them into one. They are both saying the same thing, but with different emphasis. Personally, I like the Orthodox approach as it puts the emphasis on relationship, on union, on communion. This relationship is what we are invited into in the icon, to participate in the relationship of the Trinity. Literally, to have our seat at the fourth place at the table. God's calling for us is into relationship, relationship with the Trinity, and relationship with one another.

To truly appreciate Rublev's Icon of the Holy Trinity, we first need to talk about icons in general. An icon is not a painting in the sense we normally regard pieces of art, although it is an image that is painted. An icon is a window out of the obvious realities of everyday life into the realm of God. Every paint-stroke has a meaning hallowed by centuries of prayer. Icons are religious images that hover between two worlds, putting into colors and shapes what cannot be grasped by the intellect. Rendering the invisible visible, icons are the visual equivalents of the Divine Scriptures. Not every religious painting can be considered an icon. Icons are religious pictures that convey inner spiritual meaning of their subject matter. The Son of God came to restore the divine image in human form. Iconography is the graphic witness to this restoration.

Background

The Icon of the Holy Trinity was painted by Andrew Rublev in 1425 in memory of the Russian Saint, Sergius, who lived from 1313 to 1392. Rublev painted the Icon to share the fruits of his own meditation on the mystery of the Holy Trinity and to also offer his fellow monks a way to keep their hearts centered in God while living in the midst of political unrest.

The Icon represents the three angels who appeared to Abraham at the Oak of Mamre and who ate the meal that Sarah and Abraham offered as they came to announce the unexpected birth of Isaac. Beyond the three angels, the three figures also represent the Father, seated on the left, the Son, seated in the middle, and the Holy Spirit, seated on the right, and the relationship that they share.

Russian mystics describe prayer as descending with the mind into the heart and standing there in the presence of God. Thus, prayer is where the heart of God is united with the heart that prays. As I hope you will see through the symbolism found in the Icon, we are indeed invited through the Icon to enter into the Divine Circle, and in many ways complete the seating at the table, and thus enter into the Divine relationship!

◆ ◆ ◆

Symbolism

The three angels sit in a circle and are representative of the unity of the Holy Trinity, the three are in fact one. The circle is not closed off but remains open, an invitation to us.

Do we truly belong in this icon or does it leave us at a distance in awe of the immense glory of God? As we gaze at the icon, particularly the table, our eyes become aware of the small rectangular opening in front, beneath the chalice. We must give our attention to this opening as it is the place to which the Holy Spirit points and it is our opening into our place at the table and our inclusion in the divine circle! I have heard it described that this rectangle represents the place of the altar stone, or the cavity within an altar, where the relics of a saint are kept. I have also heard that glue has been found in the original icon and perhaps a mirror was affixed there. Either way, by altar stone or by mirror, it is our invitation to sit at the table and enter into the divine circle of the Trinity and be a part of the Holy relationship.

The tree of Mamre, placed directly behind the Son, the central figure, becomes the tree of life. The tree is symbolic of the Cross of the crucifixion. Indeed, if we draw a line down through the tree, the Son, the chalice, and finally the rectangle, this forms the vertical beam of the cross. The horizontal beam of the cross is formed by drawing an imaginary line connecting the heads of the Father on the left and the Holy Spirit on the right.

The house of Abraham, which is located behind the Father, becomes the dwelling place of God and contains an open door, which is our invitation to enter into and dwell in the house of God.

You prepare a table before me in the presence of my enemies; you anoint my head with oil; my cup overflows.Surely goodness and mercy shall follow me all the days of my life, and I shall dwell in the house of the LORD forever. ~ Psalm 23:5-7

The mountain behind the Spirit represents the spiritual heights of prayer and contemplation and becomes a point where Heaven and earth almost seem to touch. Mountains hold a particular importance in the Bible. Moses encountered God on a mountain, Jesus was transfigured on a mountain, and in this icon, through the Holy Spirit, we are invited to climb our own mountain for an encounter with God.

In the center of the table, we see the chalice with the lamb offered by Abraham to the angels. In the icon the lamb becomes the sacrificial lamb and forms the center of the icon. The Son, in the center, points to it with two fingers, indicating his mission to become the sacrificial lamb. The Father, on the left, encourages the Son with a blessing gesture. The Spirit, on the right, holding the same staff of authority as the

Father and the Son, points to the rectangular opening in the front of the altar that this divine sacrifice is a sacrifice for the salvation of the world.

Returning to the rectangular opening, it is our opening into the divine circle and represents the narrow road leading to the house of God. The four corners of the rectangle represent created order and people from the north, south, east, and west. Again, a small cavity, a place for a box, is found in the central part of the altars of many Orthodox and Catholic churches and is the place where the relics of a saint or martyr, those who have offered all they had to enter into the house of love, are kept and represents our invitation to enter into and complete the Divine Circle.

As in all icons, colors carry a particular significance. To truly appreciate the icon with its colors, I would recommend doing an internet search, "Rublev's Icon of the Holy Trinity", and downloading a color copy of the icon. In the Icon of the Holy Trinity, the Father on the left wears a blue garment, representing divinity, and on top of that a cloak of an indescribable, almost ethereal, color. It seems to hold every possible color in the world. This cloak is fitting because the Father cannot be seen but at the same time is apparent in every aspect of His creation.

The Son in the middle wears two garments, the blue represents Christ's divinity; the dark, ruddy brown garment is the color of the earth, representing His human nature. The two colors worn together signify Christ's dual nature, and the unity of humanity and divinity in Him. Across His right shoulder, we see a gold colored band, a symbol of government, which signifies Christ's kingship.

The Spirit on the right is clothed in both blue and green garments. The blue once again is representative of the Holy Spirit's divine nature and the green is the color of new life.

I would like to leave you with these thoughts by Henri Nouwen, a Dutch Catholic priest, professor, writer, and theologian:

> *"Through the contemplation of this icon we come to see with our inner eyes that all engagements in this world can bear fruit only when they take place within this divine circle. The words of the psalm, "The sparrow has found its home at last.... Happy those who live in your house" (Ps 84:3, 4) are given new depth and new breadth; they become words revealing the possibility of being in the world without being of it.*

We can be involved in struggles for justice and in actions for peace. We can be part of the ambiguities of family and community life. We can study, teach, write, and hold a regular job. We can do all of this without ever having to leave the house of love. "Fear is driven out by perfect love," says Saint John in his first letter (1 Jn 4:18). Rublev's icon gives us a glimpse of the house of perfect love. Fears will always assail us from all sides, but when we remain at home in God, these worldly fears have no final power over us. Jesus said it so unambiguously:

"In the world you will have trouble but be brave: I have conquered the world." (Nouwen, Behold the Beauty of the Lord: Praying with Icons)

YHWH ~ THE BREATH OF LIFE

God formed Man out of dirt from the ground and blew into his nostrils the breath of life. The Man came alive—a living soul! ~ Genesis 2:7

> *Then Moses said to God, "Suppose I go to the*
> *People of Israel and I tell them, 'The God of your*
> *fathers sent me to you'; and they ask me, 'What*
> *is his name?' What do I tell them?" God said*
> *to Moses, "I-AM-WHO-I-AM (YHWH). Tell the*
> *People of Israel, 'I-AM sent me to you.'" ~ Exodus*
> *3:13-14*

The Jewish revelation of the name of God, as we Christians spell and pronounce it, the word is Yahweh. In Hebrew, it is the sacred Tetragrammaton YHVH (yod, he, vay, he). I have heard that these are the only consonants in the Hebrew alphabet that are not articulated with lips and tongue, rather, they are breathed, with the tongue relaxed and lips apart. YHVH was considered a literally unspeakable word for Jews. As the commandment said, "Do not utter the name of God in vain" (Exodus 20:7). From God's side, the divine identity was kept mysterious. When Moses asked for the divinity's name, he received only the phrase that translates "I AM WHO I AM" (Exodus 3:14).

This unspeakability has long been recognized,

but now we know it goes even deeper: formally the name of God was not, could not be spoken at all— only breathed. Many are convinced that its correct pronunciation is an attempt to replicate and imitate the very sound of inhalation and exhalation. If we take this a step further, literally the name of God is the sound of our breathing. Take a deep breath, on your inhalation hear the word "Yad he", on your exhalation hear the word "Vay he". Therefore, the one thing we do every moment of our lives is to speak the name of God. This makes the name of God literally, our first and last word as we enter and leave the world. When we are born, to be alive we have to take our first breath, or speak the name of God. When we die, we take our last breath, or we die when we stop speaking the name of God

This is what I encountered with my first attempt at praying without ceasing. To think of the name of God, YHWH, as only utter able by the sound of our breathing, was transformational for me. Now, as I go into Centering Prayer, as I go into difficult patient encounters, when I feel distant from God, … I just focus on my breathing. I focus on God's name and realize that God is with me and within my very breath!

When considered in this way, God is suddenly as

available <u>and accessible as the very thing we all do</u> <u>constantly, breathe</u>. How can we separate ourselves from God. Try holding your breath, how long can you last without gasping for air? A minute? If you're really athletic, maybe 2 or 3, but ultimately, to remain alive we have to breath, we have to return to speaking the name of God through our breathing.

A wonderful song that conveys this idea is, The Sound of Our Breathing ~ Jason Gray

The same breath that was breathed into Adam's nostrils by this Yahweh (Genesis 2:7); the very breath "spirit" that Jesus handed over with trust on the cross (John 19:30) and then breathed on us as shalom, forgiveness, and the Holy Spirit all at once (John 20:21-23). And isn't it wonderful that breath, wind, spirit, and air are precisely nothing—and yet everything? (Rohr, The Naked Now: Learning to See as the Mystics See)

So we might begin our blessings, "Baruch attah [or Brucha aht] Yahhhhh elohenu ruach

ha'olam"— "Blessed are You, our God, the Breathing Spirit of the world."

For me, YHWH as Breath of Life is not just a neat understanding of the four-letter Name, but a profound metaphor and theology of God. God as the Breath of Life, in-and-out- breath, that which unites all life, that which is beyond us and within us. (The Breath of Life and Prayer, n.d.)

Implications

· How can we separate ourselves from God when we literally speak his name with each breath?

· The first thing we do when born, as we take our first breath, is speak the name of God.

· The last thing we do, as we take our last breath, is speak the name of God.

· Simply breathing, if we focus on the now, and not the past or the future, allows us to "Pray Without Ceasing".

· In sadness, we breathe heavy sighs. In joy,

our lungs feel almost like they will burst. In fear, we hold our breath and have to be told to breathe slowly to help us calm down. When we're about to do something hard, we take a deep breath to find our courage. The simple act of breathing becomes a prayer.

• When we speak, we use our breath and carry God's Name. Do not use His Name in vain.

• We are all united with one another and with God through the simple act of breathing.

• What makes prayer distinctive is that we are not only using our breath to join the Breath, but in the very same breath are using our breath to praise the Breath.

Verses

Then the Lord God formed man of dust from the ground and breathed into his nostrils the breath of life, and the man became a living creature. ~ Genesis 2:7

As long as my breath is in me, and the spirit of God is in my nostrils, ... ~ Job 27:3

Thus says God, the Lord, who created the heavens and stretched them out, who spread out the earth and that what comes from it, who gave breath to the people on it, and spirit to those who walk on it: "I am the Lord; I have called you in righteousness; I will take you by the hand and keep you. ~ Isaiah 42: 5-6

And I will ... put breath in you, and you shall live, and you shall know that I am the Lord. ~ Ezekiel 37:6

Thus says the Lord God; Come from the four winds, O breath, and breathe on these slain that they may live. ~ Ezekiel 37:9

The Spirit of God has made me, and the breath of the Almighty gives me life. ~ Job 33:4

Let everything that has breath praise the Lord! Praise the Lord! ~ Psalm 150:6

Just Breathe

THE PHILOKALIA

"Love of the Beautiful"

David DeShan M.D.

What is the Philokalia?

"Love of the Beautiful"

Derived from two Greek words, "love" and "beauty," the word Philokalia means "love of the beautiful, the exalted, the good." It is an anthology of spiritual writings by some thirty Church fathers, ranging from the fourth to the fifteenth century, assembled by two modern saints of the Orthodox Church: St. Macarios Notaras (1731-1805), Archbishop of Corinth, and St. Nicodemos the Agiorite (1749-1809). The full title tells much about the contents of the books which constitute five volumes in English: Philokalia of the Sacred Spiritually Wakeful Individuals: Compiled from Our Holy and God-bearing Fathers, by Which the Mind is Purified, Illumined, and Perfected Through the Practical and Ethical Philosophy.

Writings Included in the Philokalia

The Philokalia consists of the most representative Orthodox ascetic and mystical treatises, starting with the writings of St. Anthony the Great and continuing with those of Evagrius of Pontus, Nilus of Ancyra, Diadochus of Photice, Maximus the Confessor, John Damascene, Philotheus the Sinaite, Symeon the New Theologian, Nicephorus the Monk, Kallistos and Ignatius Xanthopoulos, Gregory the Sinaite (who probably codified the manuscripts of the treatises of all of the above), and others. Of all the Church Fathers, St. Maximus the Confessor occupies more space in the Philokalia than any other Father.

It's Influence

The Philokalia was destined to have a profound influence on the spiritual life not only of Greece but of the entire Orthodox world.

This is how the pilgrim describes the Philokalia in the famous Russian spiritual classic, "The Way of a Pilgrim":

> *Ah, how much new knowledge, how much wisdom that I never yet possessed was revealed to me in this book. As I began to put it into practice, I tasted a sweetness I could not even have*

imagined until now. Often, I spent an entire day sitting in the forest, carefully reading the Philokalia and learning many wondrous things from it. My heart burned with a desire for union with God through interior prayer.

The English-speaking world owes a great debt of gratitude to G.E.H. Palmer, Philip Sherrard, and Kallistos Ware, for undertaking the translation of the complete Philokalia into English from the original text of St. Nicodemos in five volumes, as published by Astir Publishing House in Athens (1957-1963). The Philokalia signaled the beginning of a revival in monastic spirituality and patristic learning, a revival that is still going on today.

For those of us who are not practicing monastics, the idea of divorcing ourselves from the normal life may seem extreme. Nevertheless, keep in mind that those who practice the monastic life are called to live a total Christ-centered life or to use Christ's words "there are eunuchs who have made themselves eunuchs for the sake of the kingdom of heaven", Matthew 19:12. In spite of the audience, there are also sayings and writings that are relevant to those who are called to "remain in the world".

Also, this work is not meant to be read all at once. It should be approached like a Merck's Medical Journal: look up the things that are relevant for whatever moment you as a reader need it. The English translations make it easier to use it in this way. For example, if you are wondering about what patience is about, simply look at the index. If the page numbers are in bold, then it is a significant passage of text addressing that issue; otherwise it may appear as either one sentence or a small part of a larger context.

In first approaching the Philokalia an initial syllabus can be helpful. One suggested initial reading focuses on the following:

1. Volume 1, St. Isaiah the Solitary, On Guarding the Intellect: 27 Texts

2. Volume 4, St Nikephoros the Monk, On Watchfulness and the Guarding of the Heart

3. Volume 5 (Not yet released in English), Sts. Kallistos & Ignatios, Directions to Hesychasts. Although Volume 5 has not been released yet the English translation from the Russian can be found in, "Writings from the Philokalia: On Prayer of the Heart"

4. Volume 1, St. Hesychios, On Watchfulness and Holiness

5. Volume 1, Evagrios the Solitary, On Prayer: 153 Texts

6. Volume 2, A Discourse on Abba Philimon

7. Volume 1, St. John Cassian, On the Holy Fathers of Sketis and on Discrimination

8. Volume 4, St. Symeon the New Theologian, On Faith and On the Three Methods of Prayer

9. Volume 4, St. Gregory Palamas, In Defense of Those Who Devoutly Practice a Life of Stillness

10. Volume 4, St. Gregory of Sinai, On the Signs and Grace of Delusions

◆ ◆ ◆

Excerpts from the Philokalia:

Below are a few brief excerpts from the Philokalia. Many of the excerpts make excellent material for Lectio Divina and meditation on throughout the day.

St. Anthony the Great, "On the Character of Men and the Virtuous Life: One Hundred and Seventy Texts" - The Philokalia: The Complete Text (Vol. 1)

The truly intelligent man pursues one sole objective: to obey and to conform to the God of all. With this single aim in view, he disciplines his soul, and whatever he may encounter in the course of his life, he gives thanks to God for the compass and depth of His providential ordering of all things. For it is absurd to be grateful to doctors who give us bitter and unpleasant medicines to cure our bodies, and yet to be ungrateful to God for what appears to us to be harsh, not grasping that all we encounter is for our benefit and in accordance with His providence. For knowledge of God and faith in Him is the salvation and perfection of the soul.

Men are often called intelligent wrongly. Intelligent men are not those who are erudite in the sayings and books of the wise men of old, but those who have an intelligent soul and can discriminate between good and evil. They avoid what is sinful and harms the soul; and with deep gratitude to God they resolutely adhere by dint of practice to what is good and benefits the soul. These men alone should truly be called intelligent.

◆ ◆ ◆

St. Maximos the Confessor, "Four Hundred Texts on Love" - The Philokalia: The Complete Text (Vol. 2)

The person who loves God cannot help loving every man as himself, even though he is grieved by the passions of those who are not yet purified. But when they amend their lives, his delight is indescribable and knows no bounds.

The person who loves God values knowledge of God more than anything created by God, and pursues such knowledge ardently and ceaselessly.

◆ ◆ ◆

St. Thalassios the Libyan, "On Love, Self Control and Life in Accordance with the Intellect" - The Philokalia: the Complete Text (Vol. 2)

It is not difficult to get rid of material things if you so desire; but only with great effort will you be able to get rid of thoughts about them...

The first renunciation is that of material things, the second that of the passions, the third that of ignorance.

◆ ◆ ◆

St. Peter of Damaskos, "Twenty-Four Discourses", XXII Joy - The Philokalia: The Complete Text (Vol.3)

In the words of the psalmist, 'As you lie in bed, repent of what you say in your heart' (Ps. 4:4 LXX), that is, repent in the stillness of the night, remembering the lapses that occurred in the confusion of the day and disciplining yourself in hymns and spiritual songs (cf. Col. 3:16) – in other words, teaching yourself to persist in prayer and psalmody through attentive meditation on what you read. For the practice of the moral virtues is effectuated by meditating on what has happened during the day, so that during the stillness of the night we can become aware of the sins we have committed and can grieve over them.

David DeShan M.D.

St. John Cassian, "On the Eight Vices: On Anger" - The Philokalia: The Complete Text (Vol. 1)

> *"No matter what provokes it, anger blinds the soul's eyes, preventing it from seeing the Sun of Righteousness."*

◆ ◆ ◆

St. John Cassian, "On the Eight Vices: On Pride" - The Philokalia: The Complete Text (Vol. 1)

> *The thief who received the kingdom of heaven, though not as the reward of virtue, is a true witness to the fact that salvation is ours through the grace and mercy of God.*

> *All of our holy fathers knew this and all with one accord teach that perfection in holiness can be achieved only through humility.*

> *Humility, in its turn, can be achieved only through faith, fear of God, gentleness and the shedding of all possessions.*

> *It is by means of these that we attain perfect love, through the grace and compassion of our Lord Jesus Christ, to whom be glory through all*

the ages. Amen.

◆ ◆ ◆

St. Maximos the Confessor, "Four Hundred Texts on Love", 2.44 - The Philokalia: The Complete Text (Vol. 2)

> *Sometimes men are tested by pleasure, sometimes by distress or by physical suffering. By means of His prescriptions the Physician of souls administers the remedy according to the cause of the passions lying hidden in the soul.*

◆ ◆ ◆

St Maximos the Confessor, "Four Hundred Texts on Love", 2.46, The Philokalia: The Complete Text (Vol. 2)

> *The sensible man, taking into account the remedial effect of the divine prescriptions, gladly bears the sufferings which they bring upon him, since he is aware that they have no cause other than his own sin. But when the fool, ignorant of the supreme wisdom of God's providence, sins and is corrected, he regards either God or men as responsible for the hardships he suffers.*

◆ ◆ ◆

St Peter of Damaskos, "Book I: A Treasury of Divine Knowledge" - The Philokalia: The Complete Text (Vol. 3)

> *God says, 'You shall love the Lord your God with all your heart, and with all your soul, and with all your might' (Deut. 6:5); yet how much have the fathers said and written – and still say and write – without equaling what is contained in that single phrase? For, as St Basil the Great has said, to love God with all your soul means to love nothing together with God; for if someone loves his own soul, he loves God, not with all his soul, but only partially; and if we love ourselves and innumerable other things as well, how can we love God or dare to claim that we love Him? It is the same with love of one's neighbor. If we are not willing to sacrifice this temporal life, or perhaps even the life to come, for the sake of our neighbor, as were Moses and St. Paul, how can we say that we love him? For Moses said to God concerning his people, 'If Thou wilt forgive their sins, forgive; but if not, blot me as well out of the book of life which Thou hast written' (Ex. 32:32*

LXX); while St. Paul said, 'For I could wish that I myself were severed from Christ for the sake of my brethren' (Rom. 9:3). He prayed, that is to say, that he should perish in order that others might be saved — and these others were the Israelites who were seeking to kill him.

St. Mark the Ascetic, "On Those Who Think They are Made Righteous by Works: Two Hundred and Twenty-Six Texts", No. 119 - The Philokalia: The Complete Text (Vol. 1)

He who hates the passions gets rid of their causes. But he who is attracted by their causes is attacked by the passions even though he does not wish it.

The sign of sincere love is to forgive wrongs done to us. It was with such love that the Lord loved the world.

St. Maximos the Confessor, "Four Hundred Texts on Love", 3.16-19 - The Philokalia: The Complete Text (Vol. 2)

It is not so much because of need that gold has become an object of desire among men, as because of the power it gives most people to indulge in sensual pleasure. There are three things which produce love of material wealth: self-indulgence, self-esteem and lack of faith. Lack of faith is more dangerous than the other two.

The self-indulgent person loves wealth because it enables him to live comfortably; the person full of self-esteem loves it because through it he can gain the esteem of others; the person who lacks faith loves it because, fearful of starvation, old age, disease, or exile, he can save it and hoard it. He puts his trust in wealth rather than in God, the Creator who provides for all creation, down to the least of living things.

There are four kinds of men who hoard wealth: the three already mentioned and the treasurer or bursar. Clearly, it is only the last who conserves it for a good purpose—namely, so as always to have the means of supplying each person's basic needs.

❖ ❖ ❖

St. Maximos the Confessor, "Four Hundred Texts on Love", 1.24 - The Philokalia: The Complete Text (Vol. 2)

> *He who gives alms in imitation of God does not discriminate between the wicked and the virtuous, the just and the unjust, when providing for men's bodily needs. He gives equally to all according to their need, even though he prefers the virtuous man to the bad man because of the probity of his intention.*

St. Maximos the Confessor, "Four Hundred Texts on Love", 1.29 - The Philokalia: The Complete Text (Vol. 2)

> *When you are insulted by someone or humiliated, guard against angry thoughts, lest they arouse a feeling of irritation, and so cut you off from love and place you in the realm of hatred.*

St. Maximos the Confessor, "Four Hundred Texts on Love", 2.35 - The Philokalia: The Complete Text (Vol.

2)

> *Many human activities, good in themselves, are not good because of the motive for which they are done. For example, fasting and vigils, prayer and psalmody, acts of charity and hospitality are by nature good, but when performed for the sake of self-esteem they are not good.*

❖ ❖ ❖

St. Mark the Ascetic, "On the Spiritual Law: Two Hundred Texts", No. 54 - The Philokalia: The Complete Text (Vol. 1)

> *Think nothing and do nothing without a purpose directed to God. For to journey without direction is wasted effort.*

❖ ❖ ❖

St. Maximos the Confessor, "Four Hundred Texts on Love", 1.15 - The Philokalia: The Complete Text (Vol. 2)

> *If we detect any trace of hatred in our hearts against any man whatsoever for committing any fault, we are utterly estranged from love for*

God, since love for God absolutely precludes us from hating any man.

◆ ◆ ◆

HG Bishop Angaelos, "Silence is the Fastest Path to Virtue", Nikitas Stithatos - The Philokalia: The Complete Text (Vol. 4)

Sometimes silence is not indicative of a lack of things to say, but a wise withdrawal until God provides the right opportunity for response.

CONCLUSION

Prayer is nothing else than a sense of God's presence.

~*Brother Lawrence*

What would I like for you to take away from this? First of all, this is a work about my repentance and redemption. In looking at repentance I particularly like this definition: The word repentance comes from the Hebrew word, shuv, meaning to turn back, return. To return; this is the story of the prodigal son and his dad always looking for his son's return home with the opportunity to redeem his son.

Do I follow all of these daily practices or daily use every tool that I have mentioned? No! These are all things that I have found helpful over the past few years, but if I did every practice or used every tool every day, I would no longer be part of the third order monastic movement as I would have no time left for my normal life, daily work, and family. Also remember, these are merely tools and using these tools doesn't necessarily bring about union with God. We, on our own, are unable to bring about union with God. This is the work of God and the Holy Spirit; all we can do is practice being available. These activities only provide availability or repentance, an opportunity to return to or remember God throughout our normal day.

Also, I think there is a real danger in saying, "If

I do these things, I must be Holy, I must be a Holy Man!" How arrogant to take pride in seeking God by working towards humility! I particularly like this thought, "Cling to nothing, not even poverty!" How many times have I fallen victim to the trap of taking pride in humility!

So, at this time, what does my normal day look like? I start my day with yoga, which gives me physical activity to wake me up. It is also good for my bad back! I then move on to 15-20 minutes of Centering prayer. After prayer, it is easy to focus on, "How did I do today in prayer?", but this is the wrong focus. Some days, I have no problem in not having thoughts; most days it is a slog with many thoughts coming into my head. The sacred word that I most often use is "YHWH", I like combining this with my breath as it is a reminder to me that my very breath, all that I am, is a gift of God. Most days, 20 minutes, gives me multiple opportunities to practice repenting or returning to God by using my Sacred word and breath as thoughts often come to my mind, distracting me from silence. Taking me away from the presence of God. This is the point of the practice though; it is to instill the habit of returning. I then move on to some reading and/or the Daily Office. Through this, I find a thought to dwell on during the day in Lectio Divina. I often choose a Bible verse or a reading from the Philokalia, which I find a treasure trove of thoughts to ponder, I also spend some time just trying to be with Cindy and listen before heading off into my day. I am sure she will tell you though, I have a long way to go on my deep listening skills!

During the day, with encounters with patients and others, I have countless opportunities to say a welcoming prayer. Before many encounters, I use the Jesus Prayer, particularly focusing on "have mercy on us" as I find human communication is often broken and a prayer of God's mercy as we work to communicate and work together is very appropriate.

Lunch is often a time when I close my door, eat, catch up on patient charts, listen to the Midday Prayer of the Divine Office, and have 10-15 minutes of Centering Prayer.

The afternoon is filled with more patient encounters, again presenting opportunities to "See God in all". The evening allows a short time of reading and fixed liturgical prayer before bed.

The point of all of this is to have multiple opportunities to repent throughout the day, to turn my attention back towards God, see life through God's eyes, and allow God to see life through my eyes. This repenting, this returning to God, this seeing all of life at any moment through God's eyes is the meaning of "Praying without ceasing". This is what Brother Lawrence was getting at when he said, "The time of business does not differ with me from the time of prayer; and in the noise and clatter of my kitchen, while several persons are at the same time calling for different things, I possess God in as great tranquility as if I were on my knees."

How do I do every day? I am human, I have good days and bad. My temper can flare up in an instant at surprising times. What I have found though, these times occur less, they become less severe, but my old man still lives. I have also grown less judgmental of myself and of others and less surprised when my sin nature boils to the forefront. Finally, I also worry less about where I am on the journey. That is up to God. All I can do is do my part, focus on my practices, and try to live each moment as a gift from God.

If you have made it to this point and you are interested in learning more. I would suggest starting with the Trilogy of books by Martin Laird: Into the Silent Land, A Sunlit Absence, and An Ocean of Light. In the first book, Into the Silent Land, at the end of the book is a short tale, "Who am I, a Tale of Monastic Failure" which is well worth reading. For me, it is a profound tale about the journey of being human and seeking after God.

Finally, the next section, Delving Deeper, is a list of other resources to help you in this contemplative journey. All I can say is consider it a journey worth taking, following this path that God may lay before you, as you "work out your salvation with fear and trembling" before Him.

> *He does not ask much of us, merely a thought of Him from time to time, a little act of adoration, sometimes to ask for His grace, sometimes to offer Him your sufferings, at other times to thank Him for the graces, past and present, He has bestowed on you, in the midst of your troubles to take solace in Him as often as you can. Lift up your heart to Him during your meals and in company; the least little remembrance will always be the most pleasing to Him. One need not cry out very loudly; He is nearer to us than we think.*
>
> ~ Brother Lawrence

DELVING DEEPER

I drove away from my mind everything capable of spoiling the sense of the presence of God.... I just make it my business to persevere in His holy presence... My soul has had an habitual, silent, secret conversation with God.

~ Brother Lawrence

Silence

 Into the Silent Land – Martin Laird

A Sunlit Absence – Martin Laird

An Ocean of Light – Martin Laird

 Centering Prayer and Inner Awakening – Cynthia Bourgeault

Solitude and Communion – A.M. Allchin

Intimacy with God – Thomas Keating

❖ ❖ ❖

St Francis

Eager to Love – Richard Rohr

❖ ❖ ❖

Monastic Life

The Arena: Guidelines for Spiritual and Monastic Life – Ignatius

Video Documentary - "Trappist"

Prayer

Experiencing the Depths of Jesus Christ – Jeanne Guyon

Interior Castle – St. Theresa of Avila

The Jesus Prayer – Bishop Kallistos Ware

Contemplative Prayer – Thomas Merton

Liturgy of the Hours

The Divine Hours, 3 book series – Phyllis Tickle

Common Prayer, A Liturgy For Ordinary Radicals

DivineOffice.org

Universalis.com

Qleedo+ app

PrayAlways app

The Liturgical Year – The Spiraling Adventure of the Spiritual Life – Joan Chittister

Finding My Way Home - Henry Nouwen

Why We Live in Community – Eberhard Arnold

◆ ◆ ◆

Contemplative Life

Contemplative Life Series by Contemplative-outreach.org This consists of a two-year program with each section focusing on a particular aspect of contemplative living

Year One

Centering Prayer

Welcoming Prayer

Lectio Divina

Discernment

Forgiveness

Active Prayer

Attention/Intention

Year Two

Spirituality of Money

Contemplative Service

Silence and Solitude

Simplicity

Hospitality

Faith: An Advent Companion

Living in God – Nicholas Amato

 New Seeds of Contemplation – Thomas Merton

The Seven Storey Mountain – Thomas Merton

Falling Upward – Richard Rohr

❖ ❖ ❖

Orthodox Spirituality

Philokalia, The Bible of Orthodox Spirituality – Anthony Coniaris

The Philokalia – Approximately a 1400-page work encompassing 11 centuries of the sayings and teaching of the Desert Fathers

The Way of a Pilgrim

Laurus – Eugene Vodoazkin

The Wisdom of the Desert – Thomas Merton

The Orthodox Church – Timothy Ware

❖ ❖ ❖

The Trinitarian Nature of God

The Divine Dance – Richard Rohr

❖ ❖ ❖

Online Communities and Resources

Contemplative Outreach – contemplative-outreach.org

Contemplative Light – contemplative-light.com

Center for Action and Contemplation –
cac.org

The Third Order Society of St. Francis –
tssf.org

END NOTES

15 seconds to joy. (n.d.). Retrieved from debbiedwilliamson.com: http://www.debbiedwilliamson.com/15-seconds-to-joy/

Anonymous. (n.d.). *The Cloud of Unknowing.*

Beholding. (n.d.). Retrieved from Centomplativemind.org: http://www.contemplativemind.org/practices/tree/beholding

Bonhoeffer, D. (n.d.). *Life Together.*

Centering Prayer method. (n.d.). Retrieved from Contemplative Outreach: https://www.contemplativeoutreach.org/sites/default/files/private/center_prayer_method_2017-01_0.pdf

Christian Contemplative Tradition. (n.d.). Retrieved from Contemplative Outreach: https://contemplativeoutreach.org/christian-contemplative-tradition

Contemplative Tree. (n.d.). Retrieved from Contemplative Mind: http://www.contemplativemind.org/practices/tree

Dark Night of the Soul. (n.d.). Retrieved from olagjeilo.com: http://olagjeilo.com/sheet-music/choral-satb-accompanied/dark-night-of-the-soul-satb-piano-string-quartet/

Deep listening. (n.d.). Retrieved from csh.umn.edu: https://www.csh.umn.edu/education/focus-areas/whole-systems-healing/leadership/deep-listening

Fixed Hour Prayer. (n.d.). Retrieved from Phyllis Tickle: https://www.phyllistickle.com/fixed-hour-prayer/

God is Amongst the Pots and Pans. (n.d.). Retrieved from Cloisterwalk: https://cloisterwalk.word-press.com/2013/05/29/god-is-amongst-the-pots-and-pans-brother-lawrence/

Grand Silence. (n.d.). Retrieved from learningandtalent.inter-varsity.org: https://learningandtalent.inter-varsity.org/spiritual-formation-prayer/spirit-ual-formation-training/grand-silence

intercession. (n.d.). Retrieved from Peace Christian Church: http://www.peacechristianchurch.org/intercession/

Laird, M. (n.d.). *Out of the Silent Land.*

Laird, M. (n.d.). *Out of the Silent Land.*

Liturgy of the Hours. (n.d.). Retrieved from USCCB.org: http://www.usccb.org/prayer-and-worship/liturgy-of-the-hours/index.cfm

Media. (n.d.). Retrieved from Common Prayer: http://commonprayer.net/media

Meeting Jesus Through Hospitality. (n.d.). Retrieved from St Benedict.ws: http://www.stbenedict.ws/sermon/meeting-jesus-through-hospitality/

Merrill, N. C. (n.d.). *Psalms for Praying.*

Praying with Scripture. (n.d.). Retrieved from ignatianspirituality.com: https://www.ignatianspirituality.com/ignatian-prayer/the-what-how-why-of-prayer/praying-with-scripture

Rohr, R. (2018, October 8). *Richard Rohr's Daily Meditation.* Retrieved from Unknowing: http://email.cac.org/t/ViewEmail/d/8A609FBDCFFB-F2BA2540EF23F30FED-ED/001B2E9F7C6ABE62C67FD2F38AC4859C

Sarah, C. R. (2017, July 7). *Silence: God's First Language.* Retrieved from The Catholic Thing: https://www.thecatholicthing.org/2017/07/07/silence-gods-first-language/

Silence is Gods First Language. (n.d.). Retrieved from the catholicthing.org: https://www.thecatholicthing.org/2017/07/07/silence-gods-first-language/

St Bernard, Thomas Merton & Simplicity. (n.d.). Retrieved from anotherbenedict.org: https://www.anotherbenedict.org/st-bernard-thomas-merton-simplicity/

St Francis of Asisi On Joy of Poverty and Value of Dung. (n.d.). Retrieved from christianitytoday.com: https://www.christianitytoday.com/history/issues/issue-14/st-francis-of-assisi-on-joy-of-poverty-and-value-of-dung.html

The Breath of Life and Prayer. (n.d.). Retrieved from theshalomcenter.org: https://theshalomcenter.org/node/222

Ware, C. (n.d.). *Saint Benedict on the Freeway, A Rule of Life for the 21st Century.*

What is New Monastacism. (n.d.). Retrieved from Prayer Foundation: http://www.prayerfoundation.org/what_is_new_monasticism.htm

Williams, A. R. (2012, October 10). *Address to the Synod of Bishops in Rome.* Retrieved from http://rowanwilliams.archbishopofcanterbury.org/articles.php/2645/archbishops-address-to-the-synod-of-bishops-in-rome.

About the Author

David DeShan, M.D., FACOG, graduated from Southwestern Medical School in 1986 and subsequently completed his residency in OB/GYN at Parkland Hospital in Dallas, Texas, in 1990. Since then, he has been working in Midland, Texas, and is also an Adjunct Clinical Associate Professor at UN-THSC in Ft Worth, Tx. He is married to Cindy DeShan and has three children: Eric, Catherine, and Rebecca. He and Cindy are blessed with wonderful son's in law, a wonderful daughter in law, as well as many grand-children.

Beyond his medical practice, David had been serving as a medical missionary in Russia since 2002 with Agape Unlimited. Responding to God's Call, in 2006, David knew he was being called to full-time medical ministry. He subsequently gave up the obstetrical portion of his practice and since then has divided his time between Midland and Russia serving Agape while in Russia and in the U.S..

In 2008, Cindy and David moved the U.S. headquarters of Agape Unlimited to Midland, Texas, and in 2011 David assumed the role of President of Agape Unlimited.

Made in the USA
Monee, IL
28 May 2021

69701559R00115